BECAUSE *HE* SAVED ME

AMY MORTON

ISBN 978-1-0980-5497-7 (paperback)
ISBN 978-1-0980-5498-4 (digital)

Christian Faith Publishing, Inc.
832 Park Avenue
Meadville, PA 16335
www.christianfaithpublishing.com

Printed in the United States of America

For Cora
The sweetest sound I've ever heard is your two-
year-old voice singing "Jesus Loves Me."
Never stop singing for Him because He
will never stop singing for you.

Contents

Prayer

Dear God, I know that without You, nothing would be possible, and I am nothing without You. To You I give thanks for everything. I take credit for nothing and give all recognition and praise to You. Thank You for being a gracious and wondrous God, for loving Your children unconditionally, for sending Your Son to save our souls, and for giving us the strength and wisdom to complete Your will.

All of the glory goes to You, my Heavenly Father. I am saddened to think about what my life would be like without Your grace and the love of Your Son, Jesus Christ. How did I ever make it through life without the guidance of the Holy Spirit?

I pray for the Holy Spirit to work through me in writing this testimony. I have been amazed by You, and I pray that our story will praise You as You deserve.

Thank You for laying it upon my heart to write and for being patient with me as I grow toward becoming the Christian You know I can be. I know that You have a plan, and I simply pray that this book will be used according to Your will. Ultimately, I hope that our testimony will lead others to Christ. I want our story to inspire others to accept Jesus Christ as their Savior, to walk more closely with Him, to invite the Holy Spirit into their lives, and to listen when You reveal Yourself through Your divine messages.

Please don't stop working on me. You have changed me. You took an empty person and filled her with purpose. I pray that You'll use me in the manner according to Your will.

I have witnessed Your amazing ways. To God be the glory, and praise to the above.

In Jesus's name I pray. Amen.

SECTION 1

Enough about Me

Give thanks unto the Lord, call upon his name,
make known his deeds among the people.
Sing unto him, sing psalms unto him,
talk ye of all his wondrous works.
Glory ye in his holy name: let the heart
of them rejoice that seek the Lord.
Seek the Lord and his strength,
seek his face continually.
Remember his marvelous works that he hath done,
his wonders, and the judgements of his mouth.
—1 Chronicles 16:8–12

Let me start by saying thank you for being here.

It means the world for me to share my testimony with you! These chapters are filled with secrets from my past, a detailed description of the adversity I faced as I nearly lost my husband and how God spoke to me in preparation for overcoming that adversity. You'll even find poems and songs I've written for our awesome Father. My heart flows with gratitude and inspiration, and it's all because of our gracious Lord and the blessings He has rained down upon me. My soul radiates with joy, and so with my appreciation and psalms, I will sing praises to Him!

Every word in this book is inspired by God, and I prayed for the Holy Spirit to guide me throughout writing them all. Some will read this book and be shocked by the stories of sins I committed as a young adult. I've never shared these stories with many of my closest friends and family members. Some might read this book and roll their eyes and judge me. I'm not bothered by any of that anymore.

God chose me to write my testimony and to share it with you, and that's good enough for me!

We all have scars; we're all sinners. I am not ashamed. Disappointed in myself, yes, but I am not ashamed of my past because my story is beautiful. I've been washed clean! I have been given purpose! I know the feeling of not having a sense of purpose and being lost, and I know the feeling of living under the love of Jesus Christ. Once you've experienced His wondrous and unconditional love, your entire life will change, and you will be made new. Since I am new, I guess it wouldn't hurt to tell you about the old me.

Free Spirit

Jesus died and paid the price 'cause He knew I couldn't afford
To pay my toll to save my soul
And I thank You, Lord; thank You, Lord

I've done some things that I ain't proud of; I'll probably do some more
But I'm a free spirit now, and I thank You, Lord
I am ashamed, and I hang my head as my knees fall to the floor
I am free, and I'll tell you how—it's the Lord; thank You, Lord

Some owe their soul to the company store
Some owe it to the prince of this world
Some owe their soul to the good, sweet Lord
And some ain't sure, but they gotta get sure

I've done some things that I ain't proud of; I'll probably do some more
But I'm a free spirit now, and I thank You, Lord
I am ashamed, and I hang my head as my knees fall to the floor
I am free, and I'll tell you how—it's the Lord; thank You, Lord

I don't want to dive too deep into my past because that's not what this book is about. This book is about how God has taken an ugly sinner and transformed her and then gave her a story to tell. This book is about sharing His wondrous works! This book is about how someone so small and worthless can become valuable in God's plan. So to accurately share my testimony with you, I'll have to give you a snapshot of how deplorable my life was before accepting Christ.

Hello, my name is Amy, and I'm a sinner.

I'm not perfect, not even close to it, but I am constantly amazed by the blessings that God has bestowed upon me nonetheless. At one time, I thought I was perfect. In a worldly sense, I had everything you could want. However, the Lord cleared up my rose-colored glasses and allowed me to see myself for what I really was, a sinner.

Why would God waste a second on me? I am not worthy, yet God has taken this sinner and transformed me (and continues to transform me) with wondrous beauty. If you're interested in self-improvement, seek the Lord. I am proof that ugliness can turn into beauty and emptiness can transform into fullness. There are a lot of self-help programs available in terms of our secular lives, but I have witnessed the most amazing transformation available to us. No weight-loss program or self-help book can compare to the Good News available to us all.

I was raised in a Christian family, although Christ was never at my personal forefront. During most of my childhood, I was extremely shy and did not enjoy attending church or the fellowship that went along with it. We didn't go to church every Sunday, but when we did, I was bored and uninterested.

I was a great kid in terms of behavior. My grades were perfect. I was quiet, respectful, and responsible. As I grew into my teenage years, I maintained those attributes, although the devil began working to corrupt me. Without Christ, he had an open door into ruining me.

Looking back on the decisions I made as a teenager, I cringe and shake my head at that version of myself. There is a blessing in disguise here though because with that experience, I know what I was capable of; therefore, I can work hard to get my daughter on the right path early in her life. With these scars, I have confidence to tell my story because I am proof that Jesus forgives. Feeling unworthy yet receiving forgiveness is inspiring! Also, in sharing my scars, you may just find a bit of yourself in this story.

As you read this, maybe you're remembering decisions that you made at that early point in your life. Our teenage years are critical to the fabrication of our adult lives, and despite failing them miserably, I have received the ultimate blessing. It is important to know that Jesus washes away those sins and God loves you despite your past. I've been cleansed of these sins, even the worst of them! Hallelujah! You may think that you're not worthy, but that's what the devil wants you to think. God has a different message for you: you are most definitely worthy.

As a teenager, I experimented in premarital sex, alcohol, and drugs. I lived a worldly and covetous lifestyle, committed theft, lied, disrespected my parents, and disrespected God in numerous ways. I broke commandments and laws like they didn't even exist. I made decisions during that time that still devastate me today. How could someone who looked so polished on the outside have such a corrupt heart? Perhaps the saddest thing here is that I didn't have a moral authority. Sure, I had great parents and a supportive family, but I based my decision-making on meeting their earthly expectations for me rather than the Lord's spiritual expectations. Actually, I didn't even know what the Lord's expectations were. As long as I could meet the worldly expectations laid before me by my parents, in my opinion, all else was fair game.

Don't think my entire childhood was bad. I had a safe, fun, and fulfilling childhood! My parents and grandparents are fantastic people. I'm grateful for the strong work ethic they instilled in me, and they set me up to be a responsible and successful adult. I still honor them today, and I am appreciative of everything they've ever done for me. I was an honor student, graduated high school early, and worked to pay my entire way through college. I accumulated zero student debt and had a four-year college education. They kept me safe throughout my childhood. We always had nutritious meals, homework help, pets, a large yard to play in, and loving guidance. Everything a child could ask for, I had. Even though we never had a lot of money, I never yearned for anything. I learned to work for everything and to appreciate the small things. In terms of the typical American childhood, mine was perfect. So even with loving and attentive parents, the devil slithered into my heart.

I'm revealing all of this to highlight that Jesus needs to be at the forefront of any expectation we set for our children. The sins I committed during that time in my life could have had monstrous repercussions. I look back and see that God was protecting me all along. I believe that despite my sinful actions, God was sheltering me from the consequences that were possible in my secretly wild teenage years. I did an excellent job of hiding my actions from my family. My parents never knew about most of the wildness that occurred during those years. If they had known what I was up to, they would have surely grounded me forever and stopped me in my tracks! With my high grades and positive behavior both at school and home, I had my teachers and parents fooled.

I thought I knew it all. Thinking that I was capable of managing myself like an adult, at age seventeen I entered into a serious relationship with a boy two years older than me. I thought I was cool! I was dating a "man" who had already graduated high school and was living in the real world. Then at the age of nineteen I married him. I didn't love him like a wife should love her husband. I married him anyway, not even considering the fact that marriage is a blessing sanctified by God and I would have to live the rest of my life with that choice. Everyone tried to warn me of that, but I was headstrong and foolish.

We were incompatible on many levels, although I didn't recognize it because I didn't know myself yet. I thought I would grow to love him. I was excited to play house and act like a grown-up. While planning our wedding, we sat before a pastor of a church that we had never even attended and begged for his willingness to marry us. After pleading and a few visits of premarital counseling with that pastor, he agreed to perform the ceremony. All along, I knew it was a sham. In less than five years, the marriage ended.

I hope it doesn't sound like I'm speaking negatively about my ex-husband. I want to shift the focus of negativity onto myself. I was the one who longed for entering the next phase of my life—the mature adult who has a house and car and dog, laundry and bills, the decision-making, the responsibilities, etc. I guess I was reaching toward the idea of that lifestyle so I could exit the teenage phase of my life. Maybe I thought I could escape the series of immature and reckless decisions I had been making and erase them all. Too bad it was with another bad decision. I saw marriage as a way out, and I assumed that getting married was the obvious next step in life. Through my own insecurities and lack of spiritual maturity, unfortunately, I took down my ex-husband with me.

Rather than allowing God to lead me to a partner, I disobediently chose my own. Even though He forgives, I hang my head in sorrow. In the next chapter, I will discuss more in depth how God led me to discover a partner who could support my needs both of this world and the next.

After my failed marriage, my midtwenties looked very similar to my teenage years. Thinking back on that period of my life, it is easy to see that I hadn't grown or matured at all. Inside, I was still a child. I was incapable of having a mature relationship with anyone, including myself. I was still a child while going through the motions of an adult. Divorced and newly single, my life started over at the age of twenty-four.

On the outside, I appeared intelligent and capable. I had early success in my career and was perfectly polished, with nice clothing and a sparkly façade. Yet on the inside, I was lost and struggling. I had no meaningful friendships, no relationship with God, and I hid my struggles from my family. I was defiant, knew everything, and needed help from nobody. Every relationship I had was false and shallow because I was too focused on myself and my inadequacies. I had plenty of acquaintances and good-timing friends but no deep connections with anyone. I kept a distance from my family, not on purpose, but because I was consumed with a busy schedule. My schedule was filled with selfish and gluttonous fun, always striving to feel fulfilled.

The single life was one I quickly learned to savor. I dated a lot. I have stories of ridiculousness that you probably wouldn't believe. I hardly believe them, even though I actually lived them! Dating was like an adventurous playground, and it was all so new and thrilling after my divorce.

I had a wonderful job and a large income for someone of that age. My income was used to fund a lifestyle full of pleasure and excitement. I never considered the fact that I was a raging sinner; rather, I indulged in building myself upon a foundation of worldly accomplishments. I set my importance on appearance and dressed myself in a wardrobe of new and nice clothing. I groomed myself with the finest makeup and hair-care products, refining myself on the outside instead of realizing how filthy I was on the inside. I reached toward goals of this world when in reality I needed to reach toward Christ. Jesus was something I was severely missing from my life. I was a self-righteous, immature brat who desperately needed to grow up, but in order to do so I would need to revert back into a child (a babe, actually).

During that time, I never thought that the lifestyle I was leading was wrong. I was lacking conviction of my decisions and plowed through life with a careless attitude. I hurt many people, and I am truly sorry for that. I'm throwing up praises to God that He made me self-aware of how I treated others back then, and I am thankful that I've learned from my mistakes.

You Don't Know Me Anymore

I've been living my life, and you've been living yours too
Can you believe everything we have been through?
The ups and downs, highs and lows
Where, from here, will we go?
I'm just glad that our paths crossed again

We used to be so close, then we drifted apart
Despite the distance, you're still in my heart
I have changed; you don't know me anymore
I am not the same; I'm sorry for the way I was before

I've been living my life, and you've been living yours too
Can you believe everything we have been through?
The ups and downs, highs and lows
Where, from here, will we go?
I'm just glad that our paths crossed again

Thank you for asking
I've been doing really well
I've been washed by the blood of Jesus Christ!
I am new, can you tell?

I've been living my life, and you've been living yours too
Can you believe everything we have been through?
The ups and downs, highs and lows
Where, from here, will we go?
I'm just glad that our paths crossed again

I guess I don't need to reveal all the details of my debauchery; surely, you get the gist. I won't be divulging any of my husband's dirt here. He too has a past riddled with sin. God knows every little detail. When I think about my list of sins, I imagine a very long scroll listing each one, and Jesus is graciously standing there with an eraser. For members of Christ's church, God handed over the judgement to Jesus. He forgives! Even though I know it is real, it is hard to fathom the extent of our Lord's forgiveness. I pray for mercy and lots of it, and I do believe it will be bestowed upon both me and my husband. I spent so many years stacking up sins that now I'm trying to stack up my crowns so I can lay them back down at the feet of my amazing God!

It is humbling to share my sinful history with you, and while I haven't divulged all of my dirt, just know that I have many regrets and disappointments within myself. I wish I could forgive myself as easily as Jesus forgives, and working on that is a continual process. I find peace in the Word of the Lord.

Jesus summoned them, saying, "Allow the little children to come to me, and don't hinder them, for the Kingdom of God belongs to such as these. Most certainly, I tell you, whoever doesn't receive the Kingdom of God like a little child, he will in no way enter into it." (Luke 18:16–17)

A child I was, and then Jesus took my hand to show me the way. It was comforting to be knocked down to size and to be a child again. I was a twenty-eight-year-old baby who was finally ready to grow up.

How did I find Christ? Well, I'm so glad you asked! Allow me to share with you how my husband led me to Christ, which ultimately saved my eternal life (and then how I saved my husband's earthly life years later). It's a love story in so many ways, and who doesn't love a great love story?

This story is about the love of:

- yourself
- husband and wife
- family
- mankind
- God and Jesus
- God and His children
- God and the unsaved
- Jesus and His church
- the Holy Spirit and the saved

How could it get any better? Love—that's what this life is all about. And it all stems down from the one who loves the most—God.

Let's Talk about Jesus
and the Holy Spirit

If you look at the back cover of this book, you'll see a photo of my husband Jerry and me on our wedding day. That was the best day of my life! Though our paths had been different, I believe that God has destined me to marry that man, and nothing else in this world mattered on that day.

The amount of pure love I have for my husband is endless. I know his soul. I could see straight into his heart from the very first day I met him. You may be able to tell that there is an age difference on the outside, yet on the inside we are a perfect match. When we first began dating, there were a whole lot of people who didn't think it was a good idea. Honestly, we even had our own list of reasons why we shouldn't be together, but there was one big reason why we continued our relationship—God. This was the first time in my life that I had ever heard God speaking to me.

Jerry was the first person to actively and persistently share Jesus with me. God was working through Jerry to reach my sinful heart. Rather than going out on dates, we spent most of our time on my couch discussing Jesus's teachings. I asked questions, and Jerry somehow knew every answer. A spark ignited within me, and it would eventually grow into a flame that could never be extinguished.

Later in this book, I'm going to describe how an encounter with an angel prepared me to save my husband's life. Can you believe it? A messenger of our Almighty God was in my presence. That was utterly awesome! When you think of earth as a battleground between good and evil, between angels and demons, it is astonishing that God would redirect an angel from battle to visit me. Or was a battle amid me all along? The experience that I will explain later happened *three* days before my husband's death (yes, he died yet came back to us), but would you believe that, that wasn't the first time an angel had visited me?

Early in our relationship, Jerry and I had rented a cabin in the Smoky Mountains to get away for a few days. We were relaxing and enjoying our time together when we dove deep into conversation. We had stepped out onto the front porch for a smoke break. Jerry was a smoker and had been since his childhood. I cannot recall the exact details of the conversation we were having, but I do remember having a heavy heart. We were holding each other, and as I gazed off past the porch, the most amazing vision delighted my eyes.

I saw two rectangular shapes of beaming light. The light was so bright, in fact, that my eyes had a difficult time focusing. There was no sound or movement, just two rectangles of light gleaming before me. It was an awesome glorious sight! The rectangles matched in size and brightness. Their size was much taller than me, although I could not judge exactly how tall they were. I am five feet nine inches, and they were taller than me, even as I was standing on a porch. The angels were approximately fifteen or twenty yards away from us. I wish I could describe the vision more in depth, but that was simply it—two rectangular beams of bright light. However, what I can describe was the way I felt during the vision.

I knew immediately that I was in the presence of angels, and I knew exactly why. There were zero questions as to what my vision was about. God had placed it upon my heart to be assured of His messengers and their mission. Like a direct line to my heart, the angel had delivered a message that I was in the right place and that Jerry was indeed the mate that God had selected for me. With no sound or action from the vision, I simply knew. This experience lasted for just a few seconds, and I didn't even think Jerry noticed that I was staring off into the distance. Unable to speak or act, I silently stared at the wondrous display until it was finished. The angels did not reveal themselves to Jerry. He did not see or feel the encounter.

Once the vision had vanished, an immediate sense of comfort fell over me. It was a spectacular experience that was impossible to ignore. Why God was so blatant with me, I'm not sure. I mean, how many people get to experience such a glorious event? I was unsaved at that time, although I was starting to fall under conviction, and God knew that I needed some extra prodding. He wanted me! He had plans for me! I was the one who was delaying the most incredible decision I could ever make. Later I will tell you about how I'm a major procrastinator.

I'll never know why He took such special regard for me, but I suspect that He was on a mission to spread His glory through my story and to use it to win souls.

When selecting a lifelong mate, God won't always reveal His choice in such an obvious way. Everyone is different. I want to encourage all unmarried persons to please seek God before making that serious step into marriage. He will reveal His choice to you in some way. It is important to wait for Him instead of making the decision on your own. God will speak to you and your mate and will guide you both into the right decision. Take it from someone who has been in a wrong marriage. Waiting is imperative to the happiness of both you and your mate (and your kids and your family and your friends. It's a chain reaction.).

For years I was curious as to why there were two beaming rectangles. Later I would find myself in Scripture, learning about biblical witnesses and how the story of one witness is not always sufficient in building a true testimony, but two witnesses corroborating would confirm the truth.

> Whoever is deserving of death shall be put to death on the testimony of two or three witnesses; he shall not be put to death on the testimony of one witness. (Deut. 17:6)

Under the legal standards of Jewish Law, God's Living Word made it clear that it needed two or more witnesses before the truth could be corroborated. There are many instances described in the Bible where two witnesses were used to confirm the truth, but one of my favorite examples is in Luke during the resurrection of Jesus Christ:

> And they found the stone rolled away from the sepulcher.
> And they entered in, and found not the body of the Lord Jesus.
> And it came to pass, as they were much perplexed thereabout, behold, two men stood by them in shining garments:
> And they were afraid, and bowed down their faces to the earth, and said unto them, Why seek ye the living among the dead?
> He is not here, but is risen: remember how he spake unto you when he was yet in Galilee...
> (Luke 24:2–6)

During the events of the greatest miracle to ever have happened, God sent two angels to corroborate the story of the resurrection.

God also sent two angels to meet Lot at the gate of Sodom.

> And there came two angels to Sodom at even; and Lot sat in the gate of Sodom: and Lot seeing them rose up to meet them; and he bowed himself with his face toward the ground. (Gen. 19:1)

The silence of God in my life was so deafening that it was both strange and refreshing to hear Him, and I was eager to obey. Like a child craves boundaries and parental guidance, I was hungry for that leadership and authority. Really, if the Almighty God is going to present angels to you, there is no room for disobeying any longer. You listen and do exactly as you're told.

I must have had earplugs in and blinders on for the previous twenty-eight years of my life because I now know that He was always there. I know He had His hand reached out to me all along. I know

He wanted me as His child, even when I was a ruthless sinner plowing through bad decision after bad decision. God never leaves us; we are the ones who turn our backs. The devil will use any means necessary to reduce our senses, although God makes us stronger. Through this exciting time of spiritual growth, God heightened my vision so I could see the light. He heightened my ability to hear so I could understand and obey Him. He heightened my sense of touch so I could feel His love. I then tasted what victory felt like, and I knew that I wanted to savor a life with Him beyond this world. As for my sense of smell, well, quite frankly, the devil stinks!

God was making major moves in my life. Early in our relationship, Jerry and I knew we would be married. He asked me to marry him just a few days after our first date. There was no ring or formal engagement, but we both knew we were betrothed to each other. After my encounter with the two angels, I was sure of my decision. We spent a lot of time talking, and our conversations would often lead to the Bible and Jesus. Jerry bought me a beautiful Bible, and it is still the greatest gift anyone has ever given me. He was witnessing to me like I had never heard before. God was working through Jerry to lead me to Christ, and it was working.

I fell under conviction of my sinful ways, but it would take me months to hand my life over to Jesus. I lived every day with a telltale heart and a voice inside me screaming to accept Christ. The devil was hard at work taking measures to stop me. The madness between me and the devil was overwhelming. Embracing Jesus Christ was all I could think about, yet the devil had me by the arm, pulling me back. It seems so silly to me now, but at that time I was amid a deep spiritual battle! I would argue with myself that I needed to go to church to get saved. I would be at work, fretting over the formality of getting saved; and I would plan to go home that evening, lock myself in my bedroom, and have a drop-to-my-knees conversation with Jesus to receive Him (but I never did). I could always find an excuse as to why I would delay my salvation for another day. I would tell Jerry that I wanted to receive the salvation of Christ but that I didn't know the right way to do it. My mind was so caught up in the formality of the event that I was stumping myself. How could the devil confuse me so wildly? Jerry always was, and still is, laid back and relaxed, and he would simplify the situation and tell me to just do it. Anywhere, anyway, just do it. Yeah right, was it really that easy?

Yes, it really was! After struggling for months with this decision, I was simply saved while in the shower. I guess you could say I was cleansed! The Lord overtook all my hesitations and nonsense and saved my eternal life. Victory! Ask, and you shall receive.

I'll Take the Freeway

On an ole dirt road
My soul has gotten dusty and cold
And on the highway
I'm feeling low, and I can't see which way to go.

I believe I'll take the freeway, hey!
Let's take the freeway, hey!

Lost from my travels
The pavement somehow turned to gravel
Parked in a driveway
This ain't home, and clearly, I'm not alone.

I believe I'll take the freeway, hey!
Let's take the freeway, hey!

Follow His arrow 'cause this way is narrow
Follow His arrow 'cause this way is narrow
Behold, there's a sign in front of me
And it says, "This Way is free."

I believe I'll take the freeway, hey!
Let's take the freeway, hey!

If you're holding this book in your hand and you're not saved, simply submit now and talk to Christ. Feel it in your heart wherever you are, and let go of this world's burdens. Let go of your past, of your sins, and of your lack of understanding. Let go of everything, and take the bloodstained hand of Christ right now. Just do it. It's easy! He died for people just like us! If you're looking for a sign, here it is. God gave me a story to tell and empowered me to tell it, and then somehow this book made its way into your hands. Now it's time for Him to make His way into your heart.

Accepting Christ is the single most important decision you will ever make, and you will never regret it. You will never be alone, and you will never be the same. No matter what your age is, you will be reduced to a baby again; and as a child of God, you will grow beneath His parental authority. He will groom you and guide you, and He will use you for His glory. In case you didn't know, accepting Jesus Christ as your eternal Savior is the only absolute way to receive the kingdom of God. You will not spend your eternal life in heaven without receiving Christ, but don't take it from me. Jesus said it best:

> I am the way, the truth, and the life; no man
> cometh unto the Father but by me. (John 14:6)

I was such a babe in Christ that I was unaware of just exactly what I was getting myself into. I'm going to let you in on a little secret: When you give your life to Christ, He not only provides eternal salvation. You are given another gift. It's like a special offer. With the purchase of the ultimate sacrifice, Jesus will send you the free gift of eternal life. But wait, there's more! Act now to receive the free gift of the Holy Spirit! Hurry! Time is running out! This offer is not valid anywhere else. Call on Jesus Christ now to redeem this offer and receive the Holy Spirit. Satisfaction guaranteed!

> Then Peter said unto them, Repent, and be
> baptized every one of you in the name of Jesus
> Christ for the remission of sins, and ye shall
> receive the gift of the Holy Ghost. (Acts 2:38)

You Will Know

When the Holy Spirit dwells inside of you
You will know, you will know
When the Holy Spirit dwells inside of you
You will know, you will know

When you need peace, pray
And you will know, you will know
When you need power, pray
And you will know, you will know

'Cause when the Holy Spirit dwells inside of you
You will know, you will know
When the Holy Spirit dwells inside of you
You will know, you will know

When you need to praise Him
You can pray and pray to Him
And you will know, you will know

No wonder I was feeling so good! The Lord was living inside of me! Immediately, as you become saved, the Holy Spirit dwells inside of you, comforting and guiding you through this treacherous realm of good versus evil. How did I not know this? I mean, I knew something was different. I knew I was changed and that I was stronger. The Holy Spirit will put a sparkle in your eye and pep in your step! He will provide a layer of protection around you. It is a layer that is not seen but felt. In Jesus, we have an ambassador directly to God. In the Holy Spirit, we have an advocate against the devil and his army and also a spiritual leader guiding us as we grow and transform in our faith.

> What shall we then say to these things? If God be for us, who can be against us? (Rom. 8:31)

The Holy Spirit assists you in developing attributes that you may have lacked and that you'll need to have to endure future adversity. He does this to increase our character and thankfully so because I was lacking many of the attributes that I now have or are developing today. In Galatians we are told of the fruits of the Spirit:

> But the fruit of the spirit is love, joy, peace, forbearance [patience], kindness, goodness, faithfulness, gentleness and self-control. Against such things there is no law. (Gal. 5:22–23)

The struggle is real! In all honesty, I was lacking *all* of them, and I still struggle with reaching a level of each of these characteristics that I desire for myself (and that God desires for me too). This is self-help at its finest!

I have noticed such a change in myself since becoming saved, and these characteristics accrue within me as I mature. My studies and understanding of Scripture combined with the support of the Holy Spirit has allowed me to grow into a soul that I know pleases God, and guess what, I'm still growing! He knows I am working in partnership with the Holy Spirit to achieve His will, and it is well pleasing to me that He considers me worthy. I will not stop in my journey of faithfulness and growth.

I focus on the Holy Spirit to set the stage for Section 2 of this book. That is where I describe how I saved my husband's life or rather how the Holy Spirit guided me through the most intense, difficult, and unchartered time in my life. Without the Spirit, I believe my husband would not be here today, and we would be void of this awesome story to share for His glory.

Another reason I am going on and on about the Holy Spirit is because He has had an enormous impact in my life, and from my experience, the Holy Spirit gets left out of teachings far too often. I need to spread the word of God's miraculous gift to His children! I was an outsider, an uneducated and unsaved soul, and had no idea that such a miraculous phenomenon existed. We hear of the Holy Trinity—God the Father, Jesus the Son, and the Holy Spirit—but do we, the saved and unsaved, truly understand each of Them individually? I didn't understand before I was saved and even afterward too. As simple as the concept may be for some, understanding how the Holy Spirit works is foreign to others.

Even after becoming a saved child of God, I still didn't fully understand the Spirit, although He was already dwelling inside of me! It was years after I had been saved before I fully understood the gift I had received. Even though I was lacking the knowledge of how the Spirit could (and was) helping me, I still felt His support. Once I learned and began to embrace Him, everything changed! Life was easier, and I became happier. The world was brighter and more easily understood. With my new vision I was able to identify areas in my life that needed an overhaul. I started making small changes to my life, and it snowballed into this "spring-cleaning" type event. Y'all, I can't wait to share with you how I cleared out the clutter in my life to heighten my spiritual senses and to make room for embracing the Holy Spirit. We'll chat more about that in last section of this book.

As Christians, we need to raise awareness of the Lord's ability to live inside of us. We put so much emphasis on God and Jesus that the third person of the Trinity seems to be an afterthought (at least from my perspective), but in this world, having a relationship with the Holy Spirit is critical. We can't pick and choose the pieces of God to incorporate into our lives; we so desperately need each amazing symbiotic part of the Trinity. The Godhead was designed with us in mind. To achieve His will and to be sure that His children are included in His plans for eternity, He gave us the exact spiritual gifts that we would need. Receiving the Holy Spirit is the first gift, and as long as you're willing and capable of listening to God's messages, the blessings will rain down upon you. I personally have all the tools I need to be a participant in His plan because He gave them to me, and now it is up to me to use them. I have my God-given talents and a willing heart, and I also have the guidance of the Holy Spirit. As I grow in my faith, I am constantly discovering new gifts. What are your gifts?

In the book of Exodus, God worked one-on-one directly with Moses in freeing the children of Israel from Egyptian bondage and setting up their new lives in the land of milk and honey. He laid out new rules, the Ten Commandments, and also gave specific instructions on building a tabernacle. The intensely detailed plans were clearly explained, but how would the congregation be able to complete the holy site?

> See, I have called by name Bezaleel the son of Uri, the son of Hur, of the tribe of Judah:
> And I have filled him with the spirit of God, in wisdom, and in understanding, and in knowledge, and in all manner of workmanship,
> To devise cunning works, to work in gold, and in silver, and in brass,
> And in cutting of stones, to set them, and in carving of timber, to work in all manner of workmanship. (Exod. 31:2–5)

Here, we see God instilling the Spirit first and then the necessary tools into Bezaleel. He was using Bezaleel in His plan to erect the tabernacle. God chose Bezaleel and gave him all necessary tools. As for the building materials,

> And they came, every one whose heart stirred him up, and every one whom his spirit made willing, *and* they brought the Lord's offering to the work of the tabernacle of the congregation, and for all his service, and for the holy garments.
> And they came, both men and women, as many as were willing hearted, and brought bracelets, and earrings, and rings, and tablets, and jewels of gold: and every man that offered *offered* [italics added] an offering of gold unto the Lord. (Exod. 35:21–22)

What a glorious sight that must have been to see God's people lining up to contribute their finest possessions for the tabernacle's sake. They brought jewels and gold, and they also brought linens and spices and other materials. Everything that was needed for the tabernacle and its contents was provided. God is always able to provide! Unselfishly and wisely, they gave it all. Why? Because God stirred them up, and the Spirit was working within them.

We don't know the story of each individual here, but we do know that each of them was an integral part in God's plan. They had purpose, and they used their gifts as God intended. Quite simply, God gave them the spiritual gift of understanding; and with that, they contributed to God's plan for the tabernacle. Bezaleel was given a different gift—he was given knowledge to use those materials. While Bezaleel's gift may seem more important, I see it as different yet equal in value. Could he have built the tabernacle without the materials? No. Every piece of the puzzle was just as important as the next, and that still holds true in our work today. Who am I? In my opinion, I am nobody. I'm not a Moses or a Bezaleel, but I have the knowledge to know that even so, I am an important and a necessary part of God's plan. You are too! I am not you, and you are not me, but we both have gifts. While different, we are both valued equally in God's eyes.

I may not have the largest portion of responsibility in God's plan, but I am still important. I feel like one of those souls lining up to donate their possessions, and I'm going to knock it out of the park! I am inspired by the Spirit just like they were.

I can see it now—Bezaleel passionately working with his hands and directing his team to do works they had never even imagined. The divine mystery of their guided actions must have been overwhelming. I think of the teamwork and inspiration that went into the project, and I have to smile.

> And all the women that were wise hearted did spin with their hands, and brought that which they had spun, both of blue, and of purple, and of scarlet, and of fine linen.
> And all the women whose heart stirred them up in wisdom spun goats' hair. (Exod. 35:25–26)

With God, anything is possible. Here, we see both men and women—equal in value yet different in gifts—working together to complete God's will. The Bible is filled with examples of God's people using their God-given gifts to complete His will. Here we are now in the twenty-first century doing the same thing! It is time to open your heart to God's message. What gifts will He give you, and how will you use them? Or do you already know your gifts, yet you're not putting them to use? At some point, we all need to be stirred up. We all need a spiritual awakening to get ourselves in motion. First, we must accept Christ and then wait for our mission to be revealed.

Are you weak? Are you missing the tools you need to execute God's will for your life? Do you need strength to endure your earthly struggles? I found strength in the Holy Spirit. Do you need knowledge? Do you need a force surrounding you in times of despair? Are you lonely, depressed, and lacking confidence and ambition? Do you battle addictions? Are you sluggish, lazy, lost, and without purpose? I've dealt with all of those, but I found healing in the Holy Spirit. You will be amazed at what you can accomplish when you have the mental and physical power provided by the Holy Spirit—the tools you need exist! It is only He who can help you to derail the devil from your track. Your track is destined for a much brighter space! Take it from me; I'm about to testify a miraculous story of how God, Jesus, and the Holy Spirit—all *three*—came into play in the saving of my husband's life. Without a doubt, I couldn't have accomplished such a feat without such a supreme power. The devil was there working to prevent me from living out God's will, but the power of God ultimately won, and now I belong to Him.

Derail the Devil

There is a light at the end of the tunnel
But right now, it is from a southbound train
The devil is chasing you, honey
How will you ever break the chains?

Reach out and hold His hand
He can derail the devil's plan
That train will crash right off the track
And your demons will never get you back

Your train is running on steam
From a fire burning mean
And it rages every day
How will you ever break away?

Reach out and hold His hand
He can derail the devil's plan
That train will crash right off the track
And your demons will never get you back

I want to finalize this chapter with one last thought on the congregation and the tabernacle. The book of Exodus ends with this:

> Then a cloud covered the tent of the congregation, and the glory of the Lord filled the tabernacle. (Exod. 40:34)

God loved the children of Israel. Being a jealous God, He commanded them not to worship any other gods. He reprimanded them when they began to worship the golden calf, and throughout the book of Exodus we see that He wanted His people to be close to Him and Him alone. He inspired and led them in the building of the tabernacle so He could have a holy place to be close to them. Once the tabernacle was complete, His glory filled it so He could dwell with His people. Some six thousand years later, a tabernacle exists today where you can be with God. There is a place where He can speak directly to you, inspire you, where He can lead you through adversity, and where you can seek divine help. That tabernacle is *you*!

What? Know ye not that your body is the temple of the Holy Ghost which is in you, which ye have of God, and ye are not your own?

For ye are bought with a price: therefore glorify God in your body, and in your spirit, which are God's. (1 Cor. 6:19–20)

Because God sent his only Son, Jesus Christ, to be the ultimate sacrifice, our bodies have the capability to host the Holy Spirit. Yes, the Spirit dwells in churches and places of worship, and that includes your very own body. With the miracle of the New Testament, our earthly bodies can be transformed into our own personal temples; and just like He did in the book of Exodus, the glory of the God will fill you too.

My Body Is a Temple

I'm worshipping everywhere I go
I'm singing hymnals from my soul
My body is a temple
Fellowship with my Lord and Savior
I'm trekking through this world now a lot braver
Oh, my body is a temple

When the doors open on Sunday, I'll be there
Praising God with my hands up in the air
But through the week, there will be a revival in my heart
That hasn't stopped since the day He made it start

I'm worshipping everywhere I go
I'm singing hymnals from my soul
My body is a temple
Fellowship with my Lord and Savior
I'm trekking through this world now a lot braver
Oh, my body is a temple

My body is a temple; my body is a temple
Oh, my body is a temple

I'm worshipping everywhere I go
I'm singing hymnals from my soul
My body is a temple
Fellowship with my Lord and Savior
I'm trekking through this world now a lot braver
Oh, my body is a temple
My body is a temple; my body is a temple

Even though I sometimes credit Jerry with saving my life (my eternal life), Christ is the one who redeems our sins and prepares a place for us. Who is to say that I wouldn't have found Jesus without Jerry's guidance? I would like to think so, but this is how my saving story played out, and it truly warms my heart that my husband was the one who led me to Christ. What is your #savingstory?

When I am credited with saving Jerry's life, I transfer the praise to God. It wasn't me; rather, it was the power of our amazing God who made this possible. Without His love for me and His desire for me to be His child, I could have never had the power to save my husband's heart and life. With the Holy Spirit guiding me, I can do anything.

How God's Plan is Perfect

Jerry and I were married beneath a stunning Smoky Mountains sunset on a Friday in 2013. As you drive through the Great Smoky Mountains National Park on Newfound Gap Road, you will find an overlook just before you reach the mountaintop. We selected it because of the name Morton Overlook. During the establishment of the national park, the mayor of Knoxville, Tennessee, Ben Morton, personally donated funds for the creation of Newfound Gap Road. The overlook was named in his honor. Although the relation to him was very distant, we thought the name was a meaningful detail to our special day. It is one of the must-see overlooks in the park! By the way, have you ever been to the Smoky Mountains? I used to say that there's magic in these mountains, but now I see that it is God's wondrous beauty manifested through His creation.

O Perfection

If butterflies lived in the ocean, we would be deprived
Of the color and the wonder and the perfection as they fly
If cardinals lived in a desert too hot for man to go
Our eyes could not admire the perfect crimson show

O Perfection, O Perfection
How You constantly amaze
O Perfection, O Perfection
How You constantly amaze

For the valleys are green and the mountains ring true
And the skies smile down with blessings from You
The Son and the moon share in the work
Of lighting our world from the evil and dark

O Perfection, O Perfection
How You constantly amaze
O Perfection, O Perfection
How You constantly amaze

Our wedding was simple and simply perfect. I wore a long, cream-colored cotton dress, and did my own hair and makeup. I assembled my bouquet and Jerry's boutonniere. Jerry wore jeans, a white shirt, and cowboy boots. Our only witness was our photographer, and all we needed was God to bless our marriage. He did.

Two are better than one,
　　because they have a good return for their labor.
If either of them falls down,
　　one can help the other up.
But pity anyone who falls
　　and has no one to help them up.
Also, if two lie down together, they will keep warm.
　　But how can one keep warm alone?
Though one may be overpowered,
　　two can defend themselves.
A cord of *three* strands is not quickly broken.
(Eccles. 4:9–12; italics added)

The weather that day was concerning. It was forecasted to storm all day. The storms began rolling in throughout the morning and lasted into the afternoon, but they cleared in time for our 7:30 p.m. wedding. It was quite symbolic of our pasts; separately, we weathered storms for years—decades even—but now we were being joined and would have support from one another and from God to weather the storms awaiting us. The lingering clouds in the sky lent a hand unto an incredible and colorful sunset. I couldn't help but think that God was smiling as He joined man and wife. Now we were a team which, according to God's Word, is better than one; and we would be able to weather storms much more easily. Even better, a *three*-stranded cord can be pulled and weighed down with tension and stress, yet it will withstand far tougher conditions than a single- or double-stranded cord. So there we were, man, wife, and God. So there He was, God, Jesus Christ, and the Holy Spirit. A cord of *three* strands is not quickly broken.

Not long after we were married, we decided to try for a baby. We became pregnant within the first month of trying, and I was beyond elated. We kept it a secret, waiting to reveal the news until after our first doctor's appointment. That appointment was on December 27, 2013. Instead of announcing our pregnancy during Christmas, we celebrated the birth of Christ by keeping our precious little secret to ourselves. I couldn't help myself and ordered Christmas cards with the announcement on the back, but my plan was to send them out after Christmas. It was so hard to keep the huge news a secret! Christmas Day was such a special time for me. I was celebrating with my new husband in our new home, and my little peanut was right there with me. It was a day of great optimism for me as I looked into my future, seeing all of my dreams unfold. What a gift!

The day after Christmas was pure devastation for my heart. I began having cramps that progressed throughout the day, leading to a miscarriage. By the time of my doctor's appointment the next day, losing my baby was inevitable. I spent that weekend in bed in excruciating pain physically, emotionally, and mentally. Believe me, I spent a lot of time questioning God during this time. I never questioned His existence or authority, but I could not understand why God would leave me as a childless mother at this point in my life. It still hurts; however, I am at peace, and only God could give me that. He has given me answers, and I always agree that the will of God should be done. This was His plan. The love I have for that child will never cease. I'll meet that sweet soul one day as well as the soul of another baby I had lost, and this is where I'll leave this.

The year 2014 was an important year for us. We received certification for foster parenting and were devastated yet again. The foster care system is riddled with room for improvement (an understatement), but how could it not? Our country is faced with a truly terrible problem. Is it because so many have turned their backs to God? Is it a lack of regard for human life? Is it mental illness preventing parents from the ability to care for their children? Has the devil ravaged the most important and basic human organization existing in our lives—the family? The foster care system is overloaded to say the least. Through the process, we met two beautiful children, and here I am years later with a love for them that has yet to waiver. Their caseworker stated that the children had experienced the worst case of child abuse she had ever seen. Those children were abused in every way imaginable, and the magnitude of care they needed was outside of our ability. We held on as long as we could, and thankfully God put His hands on them. We were told that they would be moving to their forever home. We don't know exactly where they ended up, but I know God has a plan for them. I love those children. I think about them every day. I pray that Jesus will heal their wounds.

There are so many details from our foster care experience that I wish to share, but I'll save it for another time. I could spend hours and hours and pages and pages explaining the failings that were imposed on those children. The heartbreak compounds upon itself. I'll never know what happened to them. After they left our care, we weren't privy to that information any further. There we were again. It was Christmastime one year after losing our peanut, and we were piecing our lives back together. The first children to call me mom had vanished from my life but not my heart.

We temporarily closed our home from fostering and took time to see whether or not we were on the right path. I felt like a failure. I was mad at myself for not meeting the needs of those children. During our foster care classes, we learned how most often foster children are sent away to new homes over and over again. In and out of homes numerous times before aging out of the system, the children of our nation are continually discarded. "That would never be us," I assured myself during our training. I would never send a child away from my home! Then I did. God intervened (praise Him) and found their forever home, but I will never forget the desperation and failure I saw within myself as I told their caseworker that we needed to find a new home for them. It is extremely difficult to forgive myself, even though I do feel as though we made the best decision for everyone involved. Our hearts were broken, and we were trying to determine if this was, in fact, God's plan for us.

Sometimes God seems to leave our prayers unanswered, for His answers come in His timing. Sometimes we ask, yet the answers don't appear as clearly and as quickly as we had hoped for. Sometimes we pray for things that are outside of His will, or we become impatient in waiting for His guidance and begin making our own decisions.

Be still and know that I am God. (Ps. 46:10)

Sometimes God reveals His answers in big, bold, and blatant ways. *Three* months after temporarily closing our home, we decided to close it permanently because God gave us the gift of our daughter. We were pregnant! In 2015 we were blessed with the birth of our healthy and beautiful daughter. Praise God! We are forever grateful for His gift! She was simply spectacular! The perfect combination of her daddy and me, she was everything I dreamt about. I wish to instill in her a love of Christ and the determination to live a life in His image. Through our children, we can most effectively make a difference in this world. I work hard to set an example for her to follow and then to exceed. She makes me want to be a better person, and in turn, I can already see her excelling. I may be biased, but this little girl of mine will do great things in this life and the next.

Foster care is still strongly laid upon my heart, and I continually strive to listen to God's plan for placing such an important responsibility in my life. Somewhere and somehow, God will use me to make a difference in the lives of others. He made it clear at that time that fostering was not our path, but perhaps it will be again in the future.

For the first two and a half years of her life, Jerry stayed home with our daughter, and I worked. I had an incredible job that I just couldn't leave. He was a wonderful father, and it was a special time for both of them. Then we switched, and I was able to fulfill my lifelong dream of being a stay-at-home mom. Deciding to step back from my career and become a full-time mom was the first decision in a series of life changes that spurred my greatest spiritual growth. Life really seemed to come together quite perfectly. I had worked for twenty years ever since I was fifteen years old. My hard work had paid off! I must admit, for a few months I acted as though I was on an extended vacation. Maybe out of a deep necessity to decompress and find myself in my new role, I accomplished little and did a whole lot of nothing. I dealt with a small amount of anxiety (for the first time in my life), and I struggled to find purpose. I mean, don't get me wrong, I was loving life and celebrating every day with my sweet girl; but something didn't seem right. I knew I was missing something, and God began stirring me up. God began laying things on my heart and building up confidence within me in anticipation of something great. I'm glad I listened because I would need every shred of divine power to get through what was coming.

Have you ever worried that something big was coming and that something bad was about to happen? Have you ever felt as though everything in your life had been going right for too long and that everything was about to crumble? That was me. I knew I hadn't faced enough adversity in my life. Life was too easy; surely, it couldn't be? Adversity is God's most effective way for deepening our faith and commitment to Him. In fact, that statement comes from Dr. Charles Stanley. He has an entire sermon dedicated to growing in our adversity, and I encourage everyone to visit his website and search for the sermon "Growing in Our Adversity." Dr. Stanley points out that adversity is given, but growth is optional. "Our spiritual growth will be determined by seeing adversity as an opportunity or as an obstacle," Dr. Stanley said. Every second of every day occurs for the glory of God. Good or bad, He works through good times and bad times to allow us to grow. As Dr. Stanley so lovely stated, "Like any good father, God wants to see His children grow."

Looking back through those first five years of our marriage, life was awkward at times. We moved twice, lost a baby, became foster parents, had a child of our own, renovated a historic farmhouse, and somehow kept loving each other through it all. As I put those experiences on paper, it is easy to see how God was revealing His plan for us. It is also easy to see how some of our experiences could have gotten out of hand had we not been with a partner so perfectly suited for each other. Despite how awkward life may have been, every day was filled with love and perfection. The greatest feeling in this world is to know that you're right where you're supposed to be. So there I was, exactly where God wanted me. Boy, does He know His stuff! He considered my failings and gave me a partner who filled each of my voids. I was matched with someone whom I shared many things in common with yet offered differences that increased each of our characters. I was not where I put myself but where God's voice led me, and I couldn't have been happier. Through the ups and downs, we were always up. We were both hosts for the Holy Spirit; therefore, we were both able to give each other what we needed to fulfill God's will. I was being groomed to endure and overcome adversity and to use it all for His glory.

Without the Holy Trinity, our marriage wouldn't exist today. The track we are on could be riddled with demons at every turn, causing us to veer off course. I don't see how a marriage in these times can last without God. The devil has always been at work to destroy God's creation. Over the years, his arsenal has expanded with the rise of technology and the fall of humanity. We battle him every day, but we have an arsenal stocked with the ultimate weapons—God's almighty abilities, Jesus' eternal salvation, and the Holy Spirit's guidance through the battlefield.

> Count it all joy, my brothers, when you
> meet trials of various kinds, for you know
> that the testing of your faith produces
> steadfastness. And let that steadfastness
> have its full effect, that you may be perfect
> and complete, lacking in nothing.
> —James 1:2–4

SECTION 2

He Will Lead Us through Trials, But...

Remember the part about adversity and how I felt as though some or a lot of it was headed my way? I was right.

God had me all stirred up. I was making changes in my life, consciously and subconsciously, in preparation for adversity. The anticipation was rising within me, and I didn't know when or how. I just knew that it was coming. Little did I know that the ride would be nothing short of awesome.

In fact, I have stopped using the term "awesome" to describe mundane things. You know, that ice cream was awesome. That movie was awesome. This dress looks awesome. Nope. I love ice cream—probably more than I should—and I love movies and dresses, but those things are not awesome. God is.

God is so supremely awesome that He not only allowed me time and knowledge to prepare for catastrophe. He sent an angel to me *three* times to ensure my readiness. Allow me to share this magnificent story with you.

My mom, my daughter, and I had been visiting our family in Michigan, and we enjoyed our last evening of the trip with a family dinner at my aunt's house. It was Tuesday. We were spending the night at her home in the outskirts of Detroit because our flight would be departing from the Detroit airport the next morning. It was a wonderful week spent with family, but I was excited to get back home to my husband. I was sleeping in my aunt's guest room upstairs with my daughter by my side. She woke me up at 2:00 a.m., and after a restless hour or so, I finally got her back to sleep. She was *three* years old at that time, and it was common for her to wake during the night for some mommy snuggles.

After an hour of being awake, I found it hard to fall back asleep. I was lying in bed wide awake when I heard a noise downstairs. At that time, I didn't know that it was just my aunt awake in the middle of the night with her young grandson. My mind couldn't help but wonder what the noise was, and I began to think about how I was far away from home, in a large city, and in an unfamiliar setting. What would I do in the case of a home invasion? Where could I hide? How could I fight back? Now don't be misled; I did not feel truly threatened. My mind always wanders to the worst possible place. I overanalyze everything! I lay still to listen further but didn't hear anything else, and I felt we were safe. At this point, all was well, although I did feel a bit uneasy from the thoughts that had been going through my mind. Then it happened.

I heard a thunderously loud noise descending upon me. The room was filled with a sound as though a helicopter was humming right over the bed. The weight of the noise was overpowering. Imagine an angel two to three times larger than an average human; that was what I felt lying over my body. (The coverage felt as though it matched the same height that I saw years ago during my first encounter with angels.) From head to toe, I was completely covered by the angel's presence.

Before I go further, let me say this: I do not think angels have wings. The Bible gives us no evidence of angels having wings. Despite this, most of the art and images we see of angels show them with wings. The evidence we do, in fact, have from the Bible is that angels can take on different forms and that they most often reflect an image of man. Knowing this, it is still easy for my mind to picture a glorious angel with large, commanding wings. Picturing an angel this way was the only way for my mind to make sense of the sound I heard and the vibrations I felt during my visit.

For a moment, pretend that angels do have wings. Now imagine such a large angel with his wings flapping swiftly as he lay over me, shielding my body; that is the best way for me to describe the sound *and* the feel. I felt the vibration of the powerful wings as they fluttered above me. To me, it felt as though the entire bed was shaking. It was magnificent!

I could not hear anything through the thunderous hums. I could not lift my head, and I could not open my eyes, although I wasn't struggling to do so. I was content right as I was in the comfort of an angel. The feeling was the most comforting feeling I had ever experienced. Like the angelic experience I had encountered years ago, I knew what was happening. I knew I was among angels. God leaves no room for doubt during a time like that.

I assumed that the angelic visit lasted approximately thirty seconds, although how could I really tell? Keeping time was the least of my concerns at that moment, but I estimate it to be about thirty seconds. I opened my eyes and was stunned to see my daughter fast asleep. How could she not have woken during the noise and the vibrations? It felt like an earthquake just moments ago! She must have been deprived of the encounter. I glanced around the room to see everything as it was before the angel's visit. The room was still and dark amid a slight glow from the television. I had fallen asleep with it on and had been watching it yet again after my daughter had fallen back asleep, although now the screen was blank and had a yellow-green color to it with no sound.

I had just shut my eyes to fully immerse myself in what had just happened when a second visit occurred. Again, I experienced the same sound and sensation as the first visit. It was exhilarating to say the least. There were no words to properly describe the pure awesomeness I was experiencing! Like the first visit, I was unable to move while the angel had me covered. This time, the visit lasted maybe twenty seconds. I could tell that this visit was a little shorter, but again, how can someone keep time during such an occasion?

Once the second visit subsided, I opened my eyes and lifted my head to look around the room. Again, my daughter was still asleep and everything in the room was untouched.

I marveled at the majestic splendor of it all. I was giddy at 3:00 a.m., lying there, astonished that God had given me such a gift! Mere seconds had passed when a third visit began, and again I was covered completely. The same vibrations pulsated over my body, and the same thunderously loud hums danced throughout my ears. This third visit was the shortest in length with what I estimate to be about ten seconds.

Either *three* different angels visited me, or the same angel visited me *three* times. I cannot be sure, but either way I received an amazing blessing that night. Even though I understood the magnitude of what I had experienced, I didn't fully know the reason why I had received the visit. Was it because I was feeling uneasy about the noise I heard during the night? Surely not, but what else could it be?

Tune Out

If you're listening to the devil
You'll never hear the truth
With falseness and deception
He always lies to you

If your ears are tuned to the noise
That fills our sinful earth
You'll be missing the messages
That can reverse the devil's curse

I want to hear Your voice!
I want to go where I am led
I want to see Your face one day!
After evil is finally dead
When evil is finally dead

If your mind is consumed with lust
Tune it out; tune it out
If your heart has no one to trust
Tune out the one who shouts

I want to hear Your voice!
I want to go where I am led
I want to see Your face one day!
After evil is finally dead
When evil is finally dead

Because the one who shouts the loudest
Is the one my ears can't hear
It's the One who speaks softly to my heart
That I keep near

I couldn't wait until morning to tell my aunt and my mom what had happened! I couldn't wait to tell my husband every little detail. I couldn't wait to tell everybody! I wanted to wake everyone up right then to tell the exciting story; but of course, I let them all sleep, and I waited until morning to share my experience.

Finally, Wednesday morning arrived. I told my story to my mom, aunt, and daughter over a cozy cup of coffee while we were all in our pajamas, relaxing in the living room. There were four adults and two children in that house when the angels visited me, but not one other person heard the noise. Can you imagine what it would sound like to lie underneath a helicopter as the propellers whipped around again and again or even what it sounds like to stand near a running helicopter? I've ridden on a helicopter before, and the sound is nearly deafening; yet during my angelic encounter, nobody else heard it. Wow! My aunt was awake downstairs during the time of the angelic visits but hadn't heard a peep.

Later that morning, we all got ready and headed to the airport. My mom, daughter, and I were flying back home to Tennessee; and I couldn't wait to see my husband. We rarely spend a night apart, let alone an entire week! We boarded our plane and enjoyed some candy as we waited to take off. Thankfully, the weather was cooperating for us in Detroit. (February in Michigan was not exactly a day at the beach!) However, the pilot of our plane forewarned us that we would be flying into unsettled weather in Ohio and Kentucky. We just smiled and shared our candy. For some reason we had to wait before taking off and it was just enough time for my daughter to drift off for a nap. In just a few minutes, I would be glad she was asleep!

Not long after we departed Detroit, we met the weather that our pilot had mentioned. The turbulence was outrageous, and I was terrified! I had never ever been so scared on a flight. I made sure my barf bag was accessible in the seat pocket, and I prayed without ceasing. I cautiously watched my daughter, making sure she didn't wake up. I could barely take care of myself during the flight; I sure didn't want her witnessing the turbulence too! My mom had wisely taken a motion-sickness drug and was faring better than I was, but I didn't think the medication did much for her fear. We were all scared.

I was bouncing from side to side, wondering if our plane was about to head further south than I had planned on and thinking that maybe the angels had visited me the night before to prepare me for death. Seriously, I was that scared. I was trying to piece together exactly what the angelic visits had meant, and even though I couldn't figure it out, I was grateful that God had provided me the comfort that came along with their presence.

In case of my worldly death, I know where I'm going. I won't be dying actually, just sleeping and resting before the Rapture and the second coming of Jesus Christ. I've been saved by the blood of the Lamb, and I'm at peace with the idea of leaving this world. I'll be meeting my Savior! Nonetheless, I was watching my three-year-old daughter sleep in that airplane seat next to me and thinking of my husband who was probably already waiting for us at the airport. He's always early. (By the way, he was, in fact, already there and was watching our flight marker make its way through the weather on the map)

Obviously, our flight made it, as I'm here today to write this book. I had never been so glad to step off of an airplane! How, I don't know, but my daughter slept during the entire flight. Once we exited the airplane, she was raring to go, and my weak legs were trying to keep up with her. My husband was waiting for us, and my daughter ran as fast as her little legs could carry her before jumping up into her daddy's arms for a big squeeze. My heart was full seeing them together, but I could tell that he wasn't feeling well. I know that man better than myself, and I could see it in his eyes and body language. Something wasn't right.

We made it to our truck, and before he backed out of the parking spot, I began to tell him about the angels. The words flowed from my mouth like a babbling stream. I was full of a never-ending trickle of joy as I described what I had experienced. My heart fluttered as I recounted the details, and while I was eager to spill every last detail, I couldn't help but be concerned that he wasn't feeling well. He was listening and seemed genuinely interested in the story, but he was focusing most of his energy on acting as though everything was fine with him.

When my husband doesn't feel well, he will act like nothing is wrong. Why do men do that? I'd ask dozens of times, and he'd cringe as I spoke the words, "What's wrong?" You'd think that after nearly six years of marriage, I would be used to it. It was a common occurrence for him to not feel well, and with the history of his heart health, I worried with good reason. I never let my guard down when it come to his health.

At the request of our daughter, we stopped for dinner at a restaurant that had macaroni and cheese, Cracker Barrel. I had chicken and dumplings, and Jerry had catfish. It feels funny to think back on that dinner and how naïve to the impending doom I was. Less than a week later, I would be using Jerry's dinner choice of catfish to test his memory. We headed home and went straight to bed. He didn't feel well, and I was tired from the flight.

Thursday was like any other day. Jerry went to work, and I spent the morning cuddling in bed with coffee and my daughter. I was glad to be home and in the comfort of my own bed. Later, Jerry came home from work, and we had a relaxing evening at home.

Friday was also like any other day, at least that's how it started. Again, Jerry went to work while my daughter and I got ready for a busy day of cleaning and grocery shopping. My plan was to stock the fridge with ingredients to use for some new recipes over the weekend. During our trip to Michigan, I had been inspired to try new dishes. I hadn't even showered yet, but we went grocery shopping that morning and then spent the afternoon cleaning and unpacking the goodies from our trip. I had our souvenirs laid out for Jerry to see when he got home from work.

Jerry arrived home from work and walked in looking like a wet kitten caught in a storm. It had been cold and rainy all day. The extended forecast showed rain and lots of it for every single day ahead of us for the next seven days. I wouldn't be out in the world to witness it, but East Tennessee experienced unprecedented flooding during those seven days. Friday was just the start of the peril.

I was very proud of myself for the dinner I had prepared. Meatballs are a specialty of mine, and I had worked toward perfecting my recipe for years. After researching recipes, I concocted what I believed to be the best meatballs I'd ever made. Since my husband isn't a fan of tomato-based sauces, I had prepared mushroom gravy to simmer them in, as well as peas and real mashed potatoes to serve them with. Delicious! It was Friday, and I was ready to spend a weekend at home with my husband. Waiting for him to come home for dinner was like a kid waiting for Christmas, but his first request upon arriving home was to shower and put on dry clothes.

He was taking forever! I didn't think he had ever taken such a long shower. On top of that, I could hear him clipping his nails after his shower. The nerve of him to spend time clipping his nails when dinner was hot and ready! I could hear every little clip through the wall between the bathroom and the kitchen. I waited patiently as long as I could and then gave in. I fixed both of our plates and then sat down with mine. Oh boy, was it good!

I was halfway through with my dinner when Jerry got his plate. I could tell that he didn't feel like eating, but he insisted that he wanted it. Every bite looked like a struggle. I really think that if the meal wouldn't have been so doggone delicious, he wouldn't have eaten it. I practically begged him to let me put his meal up for later, but he force-fed himself every last bite.

I was ahead of the game for the day. I had given our daughter a bath before dinner and already had her in her pajamas. She was already fed, and I had cleaned the kitchen while I cooked. The only thing left for the day was to eat dinner and for me to shower. I finished my plate well ahead of Jerry and was putting my dishes in the dishwasher when I heard him yell from the living room, "Mom, I ate it all!" Like a kid who had cleaned his plate, he was proud, and I was too. The tone he said it in was playful and witty and endearing. I asked our daughter to bring her daddy's plate to me, and as she handed it to me in the kitchen, I heard a gasp from the living room.

"Mom, I ate it all!" could have been his last words. During his recovery, we both found humor in that.

God was about to bestow adversity upon me like never before, and I was fully prepared.

Glory to God, for He Alone
Is Worthy of Praise!

I have had CPR training a few times in my life, and I hope this story encourages you to receive CPR certification as well. The knowledge is a useful tool in terms of confidence and precision during a time of medical emergency. I knew what to do, yes, but was I fully capable of executing the actions perfectly and in a life-saving capacity? What I really want to encourage you to receive is the Holy Spirit because even with knowing CPR, I could not have executed everything as perfectly as I did without divine help. Undoubtedly, it is the Holy Spirit who saved my husband's life, and He did it by using my mind and body to make it happen.

Every time I tell this story, I am sure to make it known that it was the Holy Spirit working through me. It was the closest thing to an out-of-body experience I've ever had. I alone could have never achieved what I achieved in the six minutes I'm about to describe. I have replayed the events in my mind hundreds of times, and I still cannot believe how accurate I was in carrying out the actions that led to the saving of my husband's life.

I heard a gasp unlike any sound I have ever heard, and I instantly knew the situation was serious. With his plate and fork still in my hand, I ran into the living room to see my husband slumped over in his chair. He was unconscious and not breathing. I threw the dishes onto the floor and ran to my purse to retrieve my bottle of nitro pills. I carry them with me everywhere and have always feared the moment I would need to use them. I dumped the bottle open on the side table, plucked one from the pile, and then placed it under Jerry's tongue. At this time, our daughter asked me what was happening. I told her that Daddy was sick and that I needed to take care of him. I ordered her to sit on the couch, and she did not hesitate to comply. Bless her heart, I never want her to experience fear like that again. Her face said it all—she was scared on many levels.

His feet were propped up on the ottoman that accompanies his chair. I shoved the ottoman across the room, and his feet hit the floor. I placed my forearms underneath Jerry's armpits and surprisingly lifted him with ease. I raised him out of his chair and then placed him down flat on the floor. Thankfully, my phone was within reach, and I called 911. I put the call on speakerphone and immediately began chest compressions. I repeat, I immediately began chest compressions. The operator answered and asked where our emergency was. I gave our address and explained that my husband was in cardiac arrest. I'm not sure how much time had passed between the time I placed the call and the time the operator told me to begin chest compressions. I would think that it would be about one minute. I bring that up to say that Jerry could have missed out on that one minute of chest compressions had I not known what to do. If I had waited for the instruction from the operator, Jerry's brain and organs would have been deprived of an entire minute of blood. Instead, I began compressions almost immediately after the start of his emergency, and his body received an extra minute of life-saving compressions because of that.

The operator told me to begin compressions, and I replied that I had already started them. He asked me to count them out loud, and I did. The operator was pleased with the rate of my compressions. He told me that I would get tired but that I couldn't quit. Well, I never got tired. I was strengthened by the Holy Spirit!

My daughter witnessed every second of the entire event. She was strong too! It came to mind that I would need someone to come over to care for her because I would need to leave for the hospital. Jerry's phone was plugged into the charger and was located on the other side of his body. I told her to step over her daddy and get his phone. She yelled with fear in her voice, "I can't!" I'll never forget the terror in her voice as she said those words. She stood there next to me, petrified to step over his legs to reach his phone. Her precious little feet danced nervously on our hardwood floor. More strongly than the first time, I ordered her to do it. I told her that she had to! She mustered up the courage and did it! A three-year-old had to step over her dad's lifeless body. It is astonishing to me that she was able to do so.

My first instinct was to call my dad. I didn't even have time to think; I just called him. My dad had visited the doctor earlier that day and was diagnosed with type A flu. Praise God that he answered his phone when I called. As the phone rang, I thought that he would surely be asleep or too sick to answer; but he did answer, and he began the forty-five-minute drive to our house with my stepmom.

I saw the flashing lights of a fire truck pull up in front of our house. The 911 operator had told me that the fire truck would arrive first but that there was a paramedic on the truck and that an ambulance was also on their way. The rain from the storm that began earlier that day was drenching our town. I jumped up and ran to unlock and open the door, but then I went right back to do the chest compressions. The responders were practically wading through our soaked yard as they ran inside. They found us in the living room and swiftly but calmly surrounded me, but I did not stop the compressions until they told me to. I would not give up.

They arrived in six minutes. Later I would learn that the brain can go without oxygen for up to six minutes without receiving any damage. What an incredible blessing that they arrived so quickly!

Once they took over, I carried our daughter to our bedroom, and I sat her on the bed. I don't think I've ever hugged her so tightly. Her tiny body was tense. The ambulance arrived with a pair of paramedics. The front door remained open as the responders were in and out so frequently, which allowed our cat, Vern, to come inside. He loves to come inside but we rarely let him. He was pleased to waltz right in and find us in the bedroom. He jumped up on the bed and consoled our daughter.

My husband has three adult children from previous marriages. I called Jerry's oldest child, his son, first. It was a call I knew I would be making one day. It was a call that he feared he would receive one day. We all worried about the inevitable, and the day was upon us.

Jerry had a history of cardiac problems, and the day we all dreaded was here. His son was still in uniform from his shift with the sheriff's department when he got the call. He drove his cruiser, and I do believe that God directed traffic for him as he raced to our house. We live nearly an hour away from him. With his siren and lights, he made the rainy trip in about twenty minutes. I guess because of all that he has seen with his job, he was incredibly stoic that evening. Had he been able to witness it, his daddy would have been so proud of the leadership he displayed.

I was only able to reach one of his daughters. She was at work but was able to answer her phone. I didn't want to say the words to her, but I had to. It was a heart-wrenching conversation. His daughter is incredibly tough, and I like to describe her as a self-made woman. She has overcome many things in her life and built her own success, but as strong as she is, hearing the news put a tone in her voice that I hope to never hear again. The girl loves her daddy.

I sent a group text to Jerry's siblings telling them that he was in cardiac arrest and to pray. I copied and pasted the same words into a group text to my mom, sister, and aunts. The power of prayer was underway.

Every now and then, I would peek into the living room to see if Jerry was awake yet. I heard the paramedics shocking him with a defibrillator, and I assumed he would wake up. He didn't. *Come on. Wake up! Come back to me. I need you!* Surely, he would wake up, and then I would know that everything would be okay.

In the bedroom, I stood at the side of our bed and held my daughter's hands as she sought security under a blanket with Vern. We prayed together, and I wish I had a video of that. I looked down on her as my head bowed to God, and I could see her little eyes squinting with passion. She repeated every word I said, and her voice was beyond precious. The tone she took with God was perfect. At the time, I appreciated her maturity; but looking back, I'm astonished at just how mature she was during it all. I mean, really, she was only three years old! She saw her daddy laid out on the floor unconscious. She sensed my fear and urgency as I performed chest compressions. I had been screaming at Jerry to stay with us with a voice as loud as my voice could project. Our baby saw it all, and now here we were, one room over, listening and waiting. How did she hold it together so well? I've considered that she didn't fully understand the scale of what was going on, but she is incredibly smart. She has always shown intelligence far beyond her years. I've heard her pray before but not like that. The girl sounded as though she had a direct line to God, like He heard every syllable from her sweet little mouth. He granted an amazing comfort to her that evening.

We said amen, opened our eyes, and I just stared at her. She was petting the cat with careful and calculated strokes. All of her attention was then on that cat. I'm grateful for Vern and the way he lovingly preoccupied our daughter that evening. As I watched her, I heard my name from the doorway.

"Amy!"

Our bedroom is located right off our entryway, and with the front door wide open, there stood our pastor. I was surprised, but I wasn't surprised. Does that make sense? He has a way of showing up exactly when you need him. He lives in a neighborhood nearby and was passing our house on his drive home. I am thankful that he stopped and came inside. He could have kept driving, but he waded through the yard and the commotion and found us in mourning. Thank you, Pastor Mark!

He stepped inside the bedroom to pray with us. The *three* of us held hands in a circle and bowed our heads again as he prayed. The Spirit was definitely with us all that night! When he finished the prayer, my daughter looked up at him and said, "I heard every word you said." Oh, the preciousness! I know she heard it with her ears and also with all of her little heart.

Jerry's son arrived and walked in wearing his uniform. He acted as though he was on the call and asked for the status of the patient. The paramedics had no idea that the patient was the officer's father. They had shocked Jerry *three* times with the defibrillator before they got a very faint pulse, and they were preparing to load him into the ambulance. We live almost exactly between two hospitals; one is known to be one of the best in our state while the other is surely one of the worst for such an emergency. The plan of the paramedics was to take Jerry to the one they considered to be closer, and that hospital was the one we didn't want. Jerry's son spoke up and told them to take him to the other one, the better one—Fort Sanders Regional Medical Center. Praise God that he was there to make that call! They obeyed his command, not even realizing he wasn't actually on the call.

With my dear husband strapped unconscious to a gurney, the paramedics carried him to the ambulance through the muddy yard. As they carried him out, I wondered if that was the last time I would see his body with life in it. Could it be the last time I would be near his beating heart? Was my husband really leaving us?

As soon as my dad pulled up, I jumped in my truck to head to the hospital. I was ready to go! I had grabbed my husband's wallet, cell phone, and medications (I knew the doctors and nurses would need that information) and threw them into my purse. I did not take any hygiene items or clothing. I couldn't think any further than that night. The only thing I was concerned with at that point was making it to the hospital in time either to say goodbye or for him to wake up.

I put the truck in reverse and heard a paramedic and my dad yelling for me to stop. The paramedic didn't want me driving. Looking back on it, he was right. The rain was pouring, and I was under immense stress. Although I knew I could get to the hospital much more quickly than having someone drive me, I agreed, and my wonderful stepmom drove me to the hospital.

She did a great job getting us to the hospital, especially considering she was driving my big truck through the pouring rain across the interstate of downtown Knoxville. The potholes were horrendous!

Throughout the evening's events, I was able to remain relatively calm partially because at this point in the story, I assumed that Jerry would wake up, and I didn't know how dire the situation actually was. But because the Holy Spirit was in full force within me, I hadn't broken down. He had taken me this far, and I knew He would not leave me.

We had a private waiting area in the emergency room. I had no idea what time it was when I arrived at the hospital or how long we waited for a doctor to come speak with us. I lost all concept of time, but it felt like an eternity.

The emergency doctor, Dr. Jesse Dooers, finally came in to give us an update. He was not optimistic. I do give him credit for his consoling bedside manner, but his message was one I did not expect. Jerry was extremely unstable, and the doctor basically said that there was zero chance of recovery. He informed us that Jerry had suffered from a cardiac event called ventricular fibrillation and that we would need a miracle.

According to the Mayo Clinic's website, ventricular fibrillation (V-fib) is a rapid life-threatening heart rhythm starting in the bottom chambers of the heart. Dr. Dooers explained that V-fib was caused by previous damage to the heart, most often by a heart attack or heart surgery. Jerry had both years earlier. V-fib is extremely rare, with fewer than two hundred thousand US cases per year and is different than a heart attack. A person who goes into V-fib experiences a heart rate of up to three hundred beats per minute. At that rate, the heart cannot effectively pump blood throughout the body, so it gives up and stops. It wasn't a problem with artery blockage; it was an issue with the electrical impulses of the heart. This was all the worst possible news, and while Jerry was still alive, we were warned that Jerry was at a high risk of going into cardiac arrest again at any moment.

To put the rarity of the situation in perspective, Census.gov had a population clock that was sitting just shy of 330,000,000 people at the time of Jerry's emergency. Yet within a year, only 200,000 will suffer from V-fib. That percentage is 0.00066667.

I felt so lost. I felt as though I didn't even exist in the world anymore. I was out of my own body, in shock.

Thankfully, I was able to see Jerry, and his son and daughter joined me. There he was, laid out on the table, hooked up to everything, and clinging to life. His body was struggling. We were all struggling. As I recount this story, I can barely believe this all happened. It is surreal to look back on how rock bottom we were.

I stayed by his side and answered questions about Jerry's medical history and gave them his medication bottles. Not much time had passed when they had a room ready in the NICU for him. I walked with him as long as they would let me and then had to wait in the NICU waiting area until they got him settled in his room. Again, I waited for what felt like an eternity.

We already had quite a crowd in the emergency waiting room. Jerry's son and his wife, Jerry's daughter and her fiancé, two siblings, and the pastor of his son's church were there. Once we moved to the NICU waiting area, the crowd began to grow. One of Jerry's best friends, who was also his coworker, arrived. My mother and sister walked in, even though I told them not to come, and it was such a welcoming surprise. I had told them not to come because it was late and raining, but they came anyway, and I really appreciated that. Then the associate pastor for my sister's church showed up. I didn't even know him, but he was there to pray and offer support. Then Jerry's other daughter arrived, and now all three of his adult children were there waiting for their daddy. There were more loved ones present with us that night, I know, but my stressed-out memory could not remember exactly who. Nonetheless, prayers were going up from that hospital. The support was unreal. It was a rainy and dark Friday night, and we had the waiting area filled. Jerry was loved by many.

Outside the hospital, prayer chains were in full force too.

Finally! The nurse came in to get me, and I followed her to Jerry's room. The situation now looked even graver. The scene looked like something from a science fiction movie or maybe a medical television drama. Jerry's body was covered with what appeared to be cooling packs. His monitors were beeping nonstop. I'd never seen so much medical equipment. There were eight IV bags running into my husband's body alongside the cords and monitors, and bless his heart, he was still clinging to life. His nurse that evening, Brandy, was God-sent. I needed her compassion. She was handed a case that probably seemed impossible, but she never gave up.

The cooling packs were the first step in what the medical team called "heating and cooling protocol," otherwise known as therapeutic hypothermia. My husband was covered in air packs that were attached to a machine. The machine looked like a room air conditioner. It had red and blue buttons where the air pumped into his packs could be heated or cooled to a specific temperature. To begin the process, they started cooling my husband down to an internal temperature of ninety-one point four degrees. Can you imagine being that cold?

Research has shown that cooling an unconscious cardiac arrest patient for twenty-four hours can reduce brain injury. A Google search will provide pages of hits for your reading enjoyment. It is truly a fascinating procedure! I'm not a medical professional and won't be able to explain this with correct terminology, but I can give it to you in layman's terms. Jerry's temperature was brought down to ninety-one point four degrees, and they would leave him there for twenty-four hours. After that, they would allow him to begin warming. That's when he could possibly wake up. We wouldn't know anything concerning his neurological status until he woke up, *if* he would wake up, and *if* his heart could make it that long.

She did a fine job of getting him hooked up to the cumbersome system, and now she was entering information into the computer. She was asking me more questions about Jerry's medical history, and she asked if he had received a flu shot for the season. I could barely talk from the shock my body was in, but I was doing my best to answer the questions. The situation was extremely dire, although I chuckled inside at that question. I answered no, and her response was, "Would he be interested in one?"

Oh, if he could've heard that! He would have either died laughing (literally) or surely would've had the perfect smart-aleck response. He was on his deathbed, suffering from the most severe and lethal cardiac event that there was, but would he like a flu shot? Now I'm not making fun of Brandy. I'm sure that's a generic question in her computer system that she was required to ask. I'm glad she did ask it. It put my mind back in a place where I could connect with my husband again. I knew he would appreciate the humor in it, and I hoped I would have the opportunity to tell him all about it.

I spent the entire night either standing by his side or sitting in the chair across the room. I couldn't sleep from watching his monitors and wondering if each breath would be his last. I prayed without ceasing. I showered him with affection, wondering if God would use my touch to calm and heal Jerry's body. While he couldn't respond,

I believed that he could hear my words and feel my touch. I rubbed his feet, arms, forehead, chest, and anywhere his skin was exposed through the cooling packs.

I squeezed his hand with no reciprocal response. Imagine holding your spouse's hand without having them hold it back. It's a feeling that I never want to feel again, and I wish I could erase it from my memory. I'm not a fan of scary movies, but I've seen a few. I even shut my eyes or change the channel when scary movie previews come on the television. I don't want that terror in my mind. Holding his limp hand was by far the scariest thing I've ever witnessed.

That was Friday.

Saturday morning arrived. Brandy's shift had ended, and Ciara took over. Again, we were blessed with an incredible nurse. Ciara was soft-spoken yet sharp in every action. Like Brandy, Ciara was a big comfort to me, and I appreciated that. After all, I was barely functioning and trying to hold myself together. Regardless of the survival chances, Ciara never showed signs of giving up.

I look back and see myself at this point as an empty piggy bank that had been shattered and then glued back together. My pieces were all there, and they all fit together, but the glue was barely holding. Any more stress and the pieces would break apart. That's when we met the pulmonologist, Dr. Michael Brunson. You could have swept me up with a broom and tossed me in the trash because I became fully broken during his visit.

Dr. Brunson proved himself to be an impeccable and dedicated physician. During our stay at the hospital, I really grew to adore Dr. Brunson, but right after his visit with us that morning, I was not a fan. His bedside manner was a "matter-of-fact" style. I understood that sugarcoating the situation wouldn't have helped anything, but I wasn't expecting his report and the direct way he delivered it.

I was standing on Jerry's right side along with his son and a few family members when Dr. Brunson came in. He told us that Jerry was highly unstable, even though he was on the most advanced form of life support possible. He explained that if Jerry were to go into cardiac arrest during the advanced life support, basic CPR would not benefit him. At best, basic CPR might keep him alive but with zero quality of life. On numerous occasions, Jerry had made it clear to me that he never wanted to be on life support. He never wanted to be a "vegetable" or have a life with zero or little quality. Instead, he would want to meet his Savior and rest in a much better place. Dr. Brunson suggested that we discuss placing a do-not-resuscitate tag on Jerry. There was little to discuss; we all knew how Jerry thought of the subject, and we agreed with the doctor. They placed a purple wristband on Jerry's left arm, and in black capital letters it read, "DNR."

As Dr. Brunson broke the news to us, my body let out sounds that I've never heard before. The sounds weren't cries, and they weren't moans. They were wrenching, weeping, gravely sounds. It was a horrific sound that I could not get out of my mind. Those sounds escaped my body as involuntary actions.

Jerry's condition seemed impossible. Both Dr. Dooers and Dr. Brunson were pessimistic to his survival. I began to wallow in the impossibility of the situation, and it was a dark place to be.

Once Jerry's temperature dropped closer to the goal of ninety-one point four degrees, he began to shiver. Shivering is the body's natural reaction to becoming too cold, and it does so in an effort to create heat within the body. Since the goal of the process was to lower his temperature, shivering could not be allowed. The nurse administered a paralytic medication to paralyze Jerry's body. This stopped the shivers and also stopped my hope that Jerry would be able to squeeze my hand. I would hold his hand and pray that he would be able to find the strength and mental ability to squeeze mine back. I would talk to him and ask for a response, but there would be none. Now being paralyzed, I knew that a reciprocal hand squeeze wouldn't happen. I would have to wait.

Right before the paralytic medication was brought in, a neurologist, Dr. Samuel Moore, visited Jerry to evaluate him. That doctor said there weren't any signs yet, good or bad. It was too early to tell whether or not Jerry had sustained brain damage.

Throughout the day, Jerry's heart rhythm was irregular. His blood pressure and heart rate were erratic. We all watched his monitors fearfully. That day was the worst day of my life, even worse than the day before when it all began. I felt like a tiny grain of sand getting tossed about in the waves of a hurricane. I felt like a baby bird falling from its nest upon a cliff, spiraling to its demise. I felt as though I was trapped in a dark tunnel, waiting for the light of an inevitable train. It is surreal to remember back to that day. When I do, those emotions come rushing back, and it's enough to bring me to tears all over again.

As bad as that Saturday was, I still had to give glory to God. He alone was worthy of praise! He was already at work revealing this miracle to the world. He was increasing everyone's faith. I had the comfort from the angelic visit that I had experienced *three* days prior. As impossible as the situation felt, the comfort was undeniable. I knew that God was working through the nurses and doctors. In such a fatal situation, they all had to act with precise perfection, and even then the chances were small. I believe that just as the Holy Spirit had guided me in performing CPR the day prior, God was also guiding them with divinity.

Later in the evening, I tried to get some sleep in the chair in his room, but mostly I would sit there and stare at him. I would bawl my eyes out until they ran out of tears. Ciara had gone home, and Ellen was our nurse for the night. She was extremely intelligent, and I was impressed by her care. I could compare her to an English teacher—kind of stern and very appropriate (you know the type). I appreciated her "appropriateness." She did everything right. She explained everything to me, and I felt comfortable with her. Ellen was the perfect combination of compassionate and realistic. I needed both.

At the depth of my lowliness, I drifted off to sleep around 11:00 p.m.

That was Saturday.

For Those Trials Make Us Stronger

At 2:00 a.m. I woke up, stunned that I had slept for *three* hours. Sitting in the chair across the room from Jerry, I stared in disbelief and began bawling my eyes out yet again. I wasn't ready to be a widow. Our daughter wasn't ready to lose her daddy. Nobody was ready to lose him. Jerry was only fifty-three years old, and it was impossible to think about him not being in our lives.

I had a little stuffed puppy with me that Jerry's sister had given me for our daughter. I named him Daddy Dog and laid him next to Jerry's hand to take a photo. In preparation for losing him, I knew I could show the picture to her when I gave her the dog, and I planned to tell her that her daddy got it for her. How was I going to tell her that her daddy wasn't coming home? Maybe this gift would help; it would be something for her to hang on to forever. Our baby girl loves her daddy greatly, and she needed him to come back to her.

I sat down and didn't know what to do next, and then I remembered that I had picked up a copy of *Our Daily Bread* from the waiting room. I pulled it out of my purse and saw a verse printed on the cover:

> Therefore if any man be in Christ, he is a
> new creature: old things are passed away; behold,
> all things are become new. (2 Cor. 5:17)

The very moment I saw that verse was a huge turning point for me. I didn't have to open that little book; seeing the cover was all I needed. A rush of peacefulness came down upon my heart and mind. The Holy Spirit was still with me. Again, I was strengthened both physically and mentally. I then had a completely different perspective. Jerry would be a winner either way. He would either go to Jesus or come back to his family, but either way, he would win!

> "He will swallow up death in victory; and the Lord GOD will wipe away tears from off all faces; and the rebuke of his people shall he take away from off all the earth: for the Lord hath spoken *it*." (Isa. 25:8)

We might lose him. Here on earth, we would mourn our loss; but Jerry would be rejoicing, and we would have comfort in knowing where he would be. Losing him would only be temporary because life is short, and I would be with him again for our glorious eternity. I didn't know how I would handle being a widowed mother of a young child, but God would take care of me, and somehow I would manage.

Or he might come back to us. I would get to look into my husband's eyes again. Maybe he would hold my hand again and even be able to speak with me. He might recover and be able to go home, and our daughter could have her daddy back! The doctors said that it would be a long shot, but I had faith. I had lots of faith! At that moment, more than ever, my faith was overflowing!

I watched the monitors as the night turned to morning, and Jerry's blood pressure and heart rate began to slowly stabilize. His stats weren't perfect, but I noticed a huge improvement!

God's power was in that hospital room.

God placed it in my heart that Sunday would be a glorious day. I was anxious and ready for sunrise. With a refreshed soul, I rested in my chair until 6:00 a.m. It was time for a shift change, so I went to the waiting area and sat with Jerry's sister. Dr. Charles Stanley was on the television, and we drank coffee and discussed the glory of God. Her faith was strong too, and she agreed that Jerry was a winner either way.

At 8:00 a.m. I would be able to go back to Jerry's room. I finished my coffee and force-fed myself a few bites of a peanut butter sandwich my mom had made me. It took me nearly twenty-four hours to finish that sandwich. A bite here and there was all I could stand. My body wanted nothing. Every bite of food and every drink had to be forced down. My stomach was too nervous to hold anything, but after the peace I had received a few hours prior, I was finally able to eat and drink a little easier. I cleaned up the best I could in the restroom and stood outside the NICU at 7:59 a.m. One minute later, I hit the buzzer, and the door opened to a new day.

Optimism was oozing from my heart. I was bursting with faith! I knew that the twenty-four-hour cooling period would be over soon, and then we would begin to learn more about Jerry's condition.

The shift change brought in a new nurse, Jason. Jason is a huge blessing in my life, and I hope he understands how special he is. He has a smile that makes you feel like he is your best friend. Jason offered a natural comfort that made me feel like I had known him my whole life. We asked a thousand questions during his shift, and he never got frustrated with us. We gave advice to him, even though none of us are medical professionals! He always treated us with respect when really he could have told us to hush and leave! He was cool under pressure. Was he working under the leadership of the Holy Spirit? I think so.

That morning, Jason would ease off the paralytic medication to see if Jerry would be able to endure the cooling temperature without shivering. I would get excited because I thought that by doing so, it would give Jerry the opportunity to squeeze my hand. I would talk to Jerry and shower him with affection. I believed he could hear me. I squeezed his hand, and it happened. I felt the tiniest twinge back! I told Jason, but I didn't think he believed me. I told Dr. Brunson, and he also didn't believe me. I told his family, and I really didn't think they believed me either. Maybe they did, I was not sure, but I knew what I felt. Jerry began shivering, and they paralyzed him again.

I held onto that twinge with passion.

The neurologist, Dr. Moore, made his rounds and told us again that it was still too early for him to tell anything, except he had one glimmer of hope. Jerry's organs all appeared to be working perfectly. That was a great sign because when the body goes without oxygen, the organs are the first to receive damage and then the brain. With his organs working so well, his brain might be good too! His vital signs continued to become more and more stable. We were watching a miracle unfold.

Jason informed me that 3:00 p.m. would be when they would begin allowing Jerry to warm back up to a normal body temperature. I couldn't wait! I just knew my husband would be coming back to me.

Some friends of mine visited me around noon, and surely, they thought I was crazy. I was all smiles! How could a woman who was possibly losing her husband be so happy? God—that's how! I grin when I think about me that day. It was like Jerry and I had our own little secret. He was coming back to us, but nobody else knew it yet. With the twinge of his hand, I knew it!

At 3:00 p.m. Jason turned off the cooling function of the machine and raised the temperature by one degree. The goal was to have Jerry's temperature rise one to one point five degrees per hour, although it could take twelve hours to get his temperature back to the average temperature of ninety-eight point six degrees Fahrenheit.

Not long after 3:00 p.m. the pastor from our church and his beautiful wife came for a visit. We were gathered around Jerry's bed, and we told him all about the cooling and heating process and how they were now warming him. Our pastor, who is quite funny, said that he was going to pray over Jerry so he could take the credit when he wakes up. Now we had all been praying since this began, but Pastor Mark's prayer was that one last call to God before the great miracle happened. At around 5:00 p.m. Jason turned off the paralytic and sedative medications, and it happened. Jerry opened his eyes!

Tears of joy! Tears of joy! Praise God! Our prayers were answered! Hallelujah!

From a coma with practically zero chances, my husband battled back and opened his eyes!

Jerry was hooked to a ventilator, and with his body being so strong, he began to struggle with all of the tubes and wires. Bless his heart, he looked terrified. Wouldn't you be? Jason turned the sedative back on, and Jerry drifted back to sleep. They placed restraints on Jerry's hands so he wouldn't be able to fight the ventilator when he awoke again. Dr. Moore came into the room, and Jason turned the sedative off again. Jerry's eyes began to open, and he successfully followed all the doctor's commands. He squeezed with both hands, lifted his fingers, and wiggled his toes. The movements were all weak, of course, but he was able to complete them all. The doctor was very pleased! We all were!

It was almost time for shift change, and everyone had left the room, except me. Jason was so kind when I asked if I could stay, but the rules were strict, and I had to leave. It was extremely difficult to leave my husband's side after his awakening. I lingered as long as I could. Jerry's eyes slowly opened, and his head turned to look at me. What a sweet sight! I held his hand and asked him if he knew who I was. He shook his head no, and my heart fell to the floor. Even though his eyes were open, I could tell that he didn't know anything.

I felt both victorious and defeated at the same time. At this point, we didn't know if Jerry would still have his mental capacity or not, and I couldn't help but worry. My husband was conscious, yes, but what would his mind be like? What did our future look like? There was no way to tell if his memory had been affected or what our future held, but God had been so gracious to us. He obviously had His hand on everything, and that was all the comfort I needed. I would have to savor the victory of today and be patient for tomorrow.

The two hours of shift change felt like two days! I couldn't wait to get back to Jerry's side. I was ready for some good ole-fashioned hand squeezing! Ellen was our nurse again, and I was delighted to see her. I got settled into my chair, and Ellen dimmed the lights for the night. I sat there marveling at the day when a panic fell over me. Jerry was still wearing his DNR bracelet.

I felt as though his chance for survival was so high now that in case of another cardiac arrest, they most definitely should fight for his life. Jerry's sister, who had been sleeping at the waiting area for the past few nights, came in to say good night. I told her my thoughts on removing the bracelet, and she told me that she and some other family members had just discussed the very same thing at the waiting lounge. As soon as Ellen came back into the room, I told her my wishes. She sought approval from the attending physician to remove the bracelet, and within minutes she came back into the room and cut it off. I held the bracelet in my hands and cherished that purple piece of plastic.

I saved the bracelet for Jerry to use as a bookmark for his Bible. What a souvenir! He will always have it as a reminder of God's power, grace, and healing.

That was Sunday.

It's All for the Glory of God

That Sunday was one of the best days of my life. Right up there with our wedding and the birth of our daughter, I can't think of a more spectacular day. And then there was Monday! God had rained down blessings on us, and to experience it all was purely awesome.

Sunday night into Monday morning was a peaceful time. I tried to get some sleep in that little hospital room recliner. Maybe I got a few hours, but my adrenaline was keeping me going. Jerry was under light sedation because he was still on a ventilator. He woke up once in the middle of the night for just a few moments. I held his hand and talked to him. He seemed soothed to have me there, even if he didn't know who I was. I still couldn't tell if he recognized me or not. The good news was that he was doing most of the breathing himself, and it looked like they would be removing the ventilator soon.

I spent most of the night talking with God. I pleaded for forgiveness for every single sin I could remember, and then I asked for mercy on the things I couldn't recall. God knows my history. He doesn't forget anything. God had been stirring me up for months leading up to this, and it was easy to see why. I couldn't have endured the situation so well without Him and the lessons I had been learning. How does anyone make it through hardships like this without God?

I marveled at God's plan throughout the entire night and didn't question anything. It was clear why God had led us down this path and had been revealing himself so vividly: it was all for His glory. We were all praying like we'd never prayed before. We were sharing our story with anyone who would listen. The doctors and nurses were blown away with Jerry's progression. Prayer chains continued, and we sent out updates with the miraculous news. The network of awe was spreading like wildfire, and God had all of our hearts burning for Him.

Jerry woke up again just as I was leaving for shift change. I told him that I knew he didn't feel well and that he didn't like being hooked up to everything, but his body was strong and healthy. I also told him that the ventilator wasn't forever. With him always being adamant about not living on life support, I didn't want him to think that I had trapped him into this as a permanent solution. I felt as though he understood everything I said. I couldn't tell if he remembered me or not, but I could tell that he definitely trusted me.

During shift change, I sent out texts with excitement for what the day would hold. I knew that it would be a miraculous day! Once I was able to get back into his room, I was delighted to see Ciara back again for another shift with us. She informed me that they would be removing his ventilator that morning. Shortly after, she stopped his sedation medication so Jerry would be awake for them to remove the ventilator. He was still restrained, thankfully, because he was fighting the tubes and wires again. Imagine waking up and not knowing where you are or why you are there, and to compound upon it, you cannot speak because you are restrained and hooked up to so many different machines. We were assured that Jerry would not remember any of it, and Ciara was right. Jerry doesn't remember.

We were asked to leave the room for a few moments while they removed the ventilator tube from his throat. As soon as his door opened, we rushed back to his side, and Dr. Brunson followed right behind us. I was holding Jerry's right hand, and his family was surrounding his bed as Dr. Brunson stood at his feet. The same man who broke my heart a few days ago now looked upon Jerry with wonder. I loved seeing the expression on Dr. Brunson's face when he saw that my husband had not only survived but was now conscious. What a pivotal moment! Would Jerry speak? How would he respond? His future was teeter-tottering right before my eyes!

In Jerry's mind, I'm sure he was wondering what in the world was going on! With a room full of his loved ones, his nurse, and the doctor, Jerry looked at me and winked. With that wink, I knew that he knew me and that everything would be okay.

With all of us witnessing, Dr. Brunson looked at Jerry, and with a loud and commanding voice he said, "Jerry, say hello to me."

For someone who had just been fighting through hospital restraints, Jerry now sat there exhausted; and with a voice as weak as a newborn kitten, he responded, "Hello to me."

Tears of joy came strolling from my eyes! The room was filled with laughter and tears. We even got a smile from Dr. Brunson! Not only could my husband comprehend the question, he could also respond by talking *and* cracking a joke. "Hello to me." We're still laughing at that one!

Dr. Brunson was quite pleased and left the room in amazement. Jerry reached toward me, and with his quiet and fragile voice asked me, "What happened?"

I did the best I could to explain the entire ordeal in just a few sentences. I certainly didn't want to overwhelm him. A few minutes had passed when Jerry asked me again, "What happened?" His short-term memory was absent.

Dr. Moore, the neurologist, came in to see the wonderful sight and to examine Jerry. He was also pleased and quite happy with the way Jerry responded to his commands. Jerry could understand everything perfectly, could move all parts of his body correctly, and could speak properly; but he could not remember anything in the short term. Dr. Moore assured us that this was normal and that his short-term memory would improve with each passing day. As for Jerry's long-term memory, he joked that he could remember what he wore in 1976 but couldn't remember anything from five minutes ago.

At first it was concerning, but after speaking with him more and more, I came to see that I had my husband back, and he was on a path to recovery. Thank you, God!

Every time Jerry would ask me about what happened, I would add a little more to the story. Sometimes I would have to change it up for my sanity. It became like a game. I knew exactly how he would respond to each detail. Sometimes I would answer the question before he asked it, and sometimes I would wait to see how he responded. I was constantly testing his memory to see if he could remember something I had just said. As the hours passed by, he became more and more curious. He would ask more in-depth questions, and I could tell that his mind was working hard to understand everything.

We discovered that not only was his short-term memory absent, but also he could not remember the Thursday before his V-fib event or the day that it happened. He could remember a few details from Wednesday—the day he picked us up from the airport—but he didn't remember which restaurant we ate at or what he had for dinner (catfish).

At the evening shift change, I hated to leave him. I knew that while I was gone, he would forget everything, and I wouldn't be there to answer his questions. He would sit there during those two hours alone and wonder what in the world was going on! Sure, he could ask a nurse, but then he would wonder where his family was. Why isn't anyone here with me? he might wonder. But then again, he would forget. Bless his heart, and God be with him.

I was anxiously waiting for that 7:59 to change to 8:00 on the big digital clock that hung in the hospital hallway. With every tick of 8:00 a.m. and 8:00 p.m., I was there to press the buzzer to get back to my husband's room. We spent the evening discussing everything that had happened over the past few days over and over again. It was glorious, and I cherished every moment.

That was Monday.

Jerry didn't rest very well Monday night, although I guess he was tired of sleeping. He had been asleep for *three* days anyway, and I knew his mind was confused and keeping him awake. He would drift in and out of sleep, and I would watch him while thanking God for the opportunity. I got a few hours of rest in too, but I mainly watched him throughout the night. Tuesday morning came around, and I left for shift change. Knowing that Ciara would be our nurse again for the day shift, I could tell that it would be a wonderful day!

I floated down the halls of the hospital, grinning from ear to ear. Heading for a cup of coffee and to get cleaned up, I entered the NICU lounge to find an elderly woman crying and being consoled by her sister. Living in a hospital for days upon days like this allows you to develop relationships with other people in your same shoes. Sometimes the stress of the situation and lack of proper rest would harbor an intense environment. It was easy for minor disagreements to get out of hand. We were all packed in that room like grungy and exhausted sardines, and we'd get sick of each other's annoying habits. Sometimes a stranger would break down in tears while sitting next to you, and you would love them the best way you know how. I learned a lot about compassion during our stay at the hospital, and that one sweet elderly lady will always stand out in my mind.

Her husband was also in the NICU, and she had just received some bad news. There was no brain activity, and she was told to make the decision of whether or not to keep him on life support. Her and her sister had been at the hospital for a few days, and I found them to be precious. They were just good ole country folk. Sometimes we had simple conversations about biscuits and gravy and then sometimes difficult conversations about our husbands and their prognoses. I saw her crying, and I sat down beside her.

Inside, I was bursting with happiness and amazement at my husband's progress, yet all the while she was losing hers. I asked her how long had they been married, and her answer charmed me. "Seventy years, and we went together too," she said. Oh my, a lifetime of love! I sat with her and spoke with her about the Lord. Her husband had been saved, and that brought her much-needed comfort. How can you handle the last phase of your life, knowing that your time on earth is coming to an end, if you don't have that security of a heavenly eternity? I told her that the whole reason we're here was to love and follow Jesus and then be called home and that her husband was a winner! He had made it! Of course, it would be hard to live without him after seventy years of marriage; but she was saved too, and that meant that she would be also called home one day. I hope my words comforted her.

I never saw her again. I don't remember her name, but I'll never forget the time I spent with her. Compassion and offering sympathy have never been my strongest suits, but I believe the Holy Spirit helped me to help her. I learned empathy from strangers who comforted me when my life was shattered. The understanding words spoke to me by strangers allowed me to see through the fog of my personal situation and to realize that other people were going through the exact same thing. We were a family, and we didn't even know each other! How incredible would it be if we were able to extend this Christlike love to others all the time, not just during times of tragedy?

As time goes on, I do my best to continue displaying compassion for humanity and the folks I meet along the path of life, but it does become more and more difficult. Life seems to get in the way, and it is a further reminder to me that I need to simplify and downsize my day-to-day routine to make space for the things that really matter.

> Let brotherly love continue. Be not forgetful to entertain strangers: for thereby some have entertained angels unawares. (Heb. 13:1–2)

When I got back to his room, he was sitting up in his bed with his breakfast. Of course, he didn't remember that I had been there, and he wondered where I had been. All I could do was smile and laugh and remind him of everything. He swore that he didn't sleep a wink all night long, even though I knew he slept for a few hours.

Friends and family visited throughout the day. We watched the local news and episodes of *The Andy Griffith Show*.

The cardiologist, Dr. Trotter, came to visit Jerry and began formulating a plan. Dr. Trotter ordered a heart cath for Wednesday morning and said that he would be discussing Jerry's case with an electrical doctor. The electrical doctor, Dr. Mehta, would possibly install a pacemaker/defibrillator if he determined that Jerry was a good candidate. We all prayed that it would happen. Jerry was scared that he would undergo another cardiac arrest. He did not want to go home without the insurance of a device, and I felt the same way.

Because Jerry was progressing so quickly, he was moved to a stepdown unit. I gathered up four days' worth of belongings and prepared for the trip down the hall. Ciara wouldn't be going with us. She was an amazing nurse, and I did find peace that she would be there in that room, ready to care for the next patient who came through. Whoever they would be, they would be in good hands! I was nervous about the move, but God held my hand and gave me a sense of peacefulness. I knew that He had a plan, and this move was the next step.

I didn't realize the weight of the high-stress environment we were in until we moved to our new room. The area that our new room was in was much more private. You had to go through two sets of closed doors to get back to that area. Our room was located at the end of the hallway. I loved the location because there was never anyone outside the room other than Jerry's nurses and doctors. The room was huge! It was like a hotel suite! We had come from a tiny room that was situated right at the nurses' station. There had been constant beeping sounds echoing through the halls and carts rolling by. The noises were suffocating, and the tiny room felt claustrophobic; but once we arrived at our new room, we seemed to be in a paradise.

They rolled Jerry into his new room on his big plush hospital bed that he received in the NICU. I had never seen such a nice hospital bed, and I was glad he got to keep it. It was nicer than our bed at home! At first, they wanted to place him in a standard hospital bed, but Ciara fought for us to keep the nicer one. Thanks, Ciara! As we strolled into the new room, my eyes immediately went to the couch along the wall of huge windows. A couch! Not a recliner like I had slept on for the past four nights, but a full-length couch that I would be able to stretch out on. Thank you, God! And the windows, let's talk about those windows.

It had rained nonstop since we had been in the hospital. East Tennessee had experienced unprecedented rainfall during that time, and it was depressing on everyone's mood to look out and see the dreary weather. Now here I was, looking out of this huge window at the sunshine! The window in our room spanned from wall to wall, and it looked out over a beautiful view of Knoxville, Tennessee. I could see houses and businesses and life! The rain had paused briefly, and the sunshine filled my heart.

We had two nurses that night, Michael and Daniel. They were both very laid back and enjoyable to be around. They took great care of my husband, but they also acted like buddies to him. They all joked around and laughed. They were exactly what Jerry needed, even though he does not remember them now. In fact, Jerry doesn't remember anything about being in that room or the room before it.

Michael showed me the kitchen, which was stocked with anything you could want during your stay at the fabulous Fort Sander's Regional Medical Center's all-inclusive resort. There was a refrigerator stocked with any kind of soda you would desire, along with milk, meal-replacement shakes, Jell-O, pudding, and other goodies. The freezer was stocked with ice cream and popsicles, although there was never any chocolate. I heard through the grapevine that chocolate was always the first to go. He showed me the cabinets and drawers filled with crackers, peanut butter, packets of honey, and other snacks. It was all so lovely, although I couldn't take my mind off of the coffee machine.

When Jerry and I had our daughter, I gave birth at the same hospital. Just down the hall from my hospital room during that stay, there was a snack area with the same style of coffee machine. When I saw that we had the same coffee machine during this hospital stay, I was thrilled! The recovery from having my daughter was tough, and walking down the hall to get a cappuccino or a coffee was a major feat. Here I was again. I had made it to the coffee machine!

I went back into Jerry's room and bragged how the kitchen had anything he could possibly want to drink, and I offered to go get him something. He thought for a moment and then decided on chocolate milk. I waltzed down the hall to the kitchen only to find that all of the chocolate milk was gone! I was *not* going back to his room without chocolate milk. I opened every cabinet and drawer, looking for anything that could be used for chocolate milk. I found hot chocolate packets and stirring sticks. I made a cup of concentrated hot chocolate, added ice, and then shook it like I was a bartender. Then I mixed it with white milk, and voila! My husband had chocolate milk. I tasted it, and it was a little weird, but I thought it could pass for chocolate milk. I walked back to his room and handed it to him nervously, wondering if he would find the taste unusual. He drank it all without saying a word, and we all smiled.

I'll never forget how luxurious that hospital room felt. God knew that I needed a little TLC, and I knew that He was comforting me.

That evening, we heard a call over the intercom. It was a warning that a LIFE STAR helicopter would be landing in five minutes and that the team attending to the call should be prepared. Daniel and Michael were part of that team, and they left briefly to tend to that arriving patient. I felt that Jerry was in good hands with nurses so accomplished that they would be a part of such a vital team.

Later on, Michael came into the room and asked Jerry *three* questions to test his memory. He asked what month it was, what hospital he was in, and who the president was. Jerry had to guess the month. It was February, but he guessed June. Jerry opened his mouth to say the name of the other hospital that the paramedics had almost taken him to. I guess it was good that he could remember that part of the story I had told him—about how he almost went to that hospital and that his son had told the paramedics to go to Fort Sanders—but his mind couldn't grasp which hospital he ended up at. Before he said the wrong hospital name, he saw the dry-erase board on the wall that said, "Fort Sanders Regional Medical Center." I watched his eyes as he tried to figure out which hospital he was in, and as they rose up to see the dry-erase board, I was grinning that he cleverly figured it out. He barely got that second question right. As for the president, thankfully, he remembered that it was Donald Trump.

It was getting late into the evening, and Jerry drifted off to sleep. I lay there, stretched out on the couch and relaxed. It was the first night in five nights that I was able to lie down. I heard another alert over the intercom that a LIFE STAR helicopter would be landing soon. I didn't think too much of it. I was in a wonderful peace lying there on the couch, and then five minutes later I heard a familiar sound.

A helicopter was humming over me. A helicopter was humming over me! I hadn't noticed it earlier during the first helicopter landing, but the landing pad must have been right above our hospital room. Wow! I must have been talking to Jerry or had been preoccupied with the noise of the day to hear it during the first landing, but now that the stillness of the night was upon me, I heard that beautiful flutter!

I quickly remembered the angel who seemingly fluttered over me exactly seven days prior. *Exactly seven days prior.* I was in such a

God-place because when that familiar sound came down on me in that hospital room, tears immediately came pouring from my eyes with gratitude. The week had come full circle. Seven days ago, I was unaware of what lay ahead of me. I had been comforted by an angelic visit for a reason not known then. Then I had lived through the lowest points in my life and experienced God's power and mercy. I had faced adversity like never before and was worshipping and praising God with every breath. After everything, of all of the places in that hospital for me to be, I was right under the landing pad for helicopters.

What a blessing!

Jerry woke up for a minute, and I lunged to his bedside, telling him everything about the angel and the helicopter. He hadn't remembered anything about my angel story from a week ago, and I had to retell everything. He was excited and amazed, although he quickly forgot. That's okay though because it was my favorite story to tell, and I got to tell it to him over and over again like it was the first time.

I returned to my couch with amazement and smiled toward the direction of the landing pad. Before I fell asleep that night, one more helicopter flew in for a total of *three* that night. You read that right— *three* helicopter landings right above me seven days after I experienced *three* helicopter-sounding angelic visits. My dear God, You are amazing, and I thank You for revealing Yourself to me through all of this.

We both slept much better that night. Every time I checked, Jerry was asleep. Even so, the next morning he'd tell me that he didn't sleep a wink.

That was Tuesday.

On Wednesday, Jerry's heart cath came back perfectly. No stents or open-heart surgeries would be needed, so with no other obstacles in the way, Jerry was ready to receive the implantation of a pacemaker/defibrillator. Both the electrical doctor and the cardiologist agreed that it was the best plan for Jerry, and it was scheduled for Thursday morning.

What a lovely afternoon! My husband would be receiving the blessing of a device that could prevent this same thing from happening again. We were beyond grateful! We were smiling from ear to ear and looking forward to another night in paradise.

Later in the afternoon, our nurse came in and said that we would be moving rooms again, but this time we would be moving down to the very basic hospital room. I dreaded leaving the lap of hospital luxury. My coffee machine, the snacks, the spacious room, and the pretty view would be long gone. (Okay, maybe I snuck back in the next day for a cup of coffee.) The long couch that made for such a comfortable bed would no longer be mine, but what worried me more than losing those consoling amenities was that we would be losing the constant care and attention from our top-notch nurses.

Our nurse went to find someone to help her move us. While she was gone, Jerry suddenly became flush and dizzy. His heart was fluttering. He was trying to eat his dinner but lost his appetite. Was something serious about to happen? I wondered if maybe this was God's way of letting us spend one more night in our hospital suite. I pressed the call button and told them something was happening to him, and two nurses rushed in. They checked the monitors and evaluated him. I was a nervous wreck! I was strong and was willing to endure anything that God laid before me, but I was also living on eggshells. The moment passed, and Jerry felt fine again. The nurses examined him and determined that he was okay. They went back in the monitor's record and saw the hiccup that his heart had just had, and they even printed the slip out for me to see. I still have it sitting on our fireplace. It reminds me of how quick life can change and how precious each beat of our hearts is.

We asked if moving was really a good idea, but our nurse assured us that he was fine and ready to be stepped down to the basic cardiac unit.

We lost all of the monitors. Jerry was still observed, but now it would be remotely at the nurse's station instead of with the in-room monitors. I loved watching the monitors and being reassured of his perfect vitals. I had found great comfort in keeping track of his heart rate and rhythm, along with his oxygen level. That comfort was gone. We lost the top-notch level of care we had been receiving from our nurses. It was obvious that the nurses who excelled in their profession were stationed in the areas of utmost importance. Now that we were stepped down into an average room, we received average care.

Our room was exactly what you would expect. Four walls, check. Scrambled television with the sound coming from the remote, check. View of the hospital's air conditioners, check. Squeaky recliner that wouldn't stay reclined back, check.

I know it sounds petty to complain about the move and about the new room. I should have been grateful that we were even in the room! My husband was alive for God's sake (literally)! I see all of that now, but at that time I couldn't help it. I was fragile. I was in uncharted waters, and I was afraid. Even with the guidance of the Holy Spirit, I couldn't help but feel a bit lost. O ye of little faith.

The Holy Spirit was still fully in charge of my life. He was with me from the start on that rainy Friday evening, guiding me through chest compressions and keeping me calm as my daughter watched my every move. He was with me in the emergency room as I waited for the doctor to speak with me. He was there through every moment, I know it, and He was still there with me in that dingy and cold hospital room.

They transferred Jerry to a standard hospital bed. Bye-bye, fancy plush bed; and hello, lumpy and awkward new bed. When they were getting us settled in the new room, Jerry didn't feel like lying down. He chose to sit on the edge of the bed for a while. Of course, there were no nurses in sight when he was ready to lie down on his bed. I had a heck of a time getting him situated. Somehow, during his V-fib event, I was able to lift all 230 pounds of him down on the floor. Now, I couldn't even get him settled into bed. From the forty minutes of chest compressions Jerry had received that Friday evening, he was in excruciating pain anytime he coughed or moved his torso. My sole purpose in life during all of this was to care for my husband. I wanted him to have the utmost comfort, and with setting my standards so high, it was easy for me to feel like a failure. Even though we were in a hospital full of professional medical caregivers, I felt that it was my responsibility to make sure he had everything he needed and wanted. After all, he was my husband, and he was the father of my daughter; and we needed him! I was determined to do anything to help him in his recovery.

Jerry was an extreme fall risk. In fact, on the discharge papers we would receive a few days later, fall risk was written five times in a row and in capital letters. He needed to use the restroom, and I did my best to help him walk there. It was only seven or eight feet away from his bed, but to him it was like a mile. My nerves were shot. An hour ago, we had all of the help we ever wanted. Now I felt as though we were abandoned and helpless.

That was a rough evening for me.

> And all things, whatsoever ye shall ask in
> prayer, believing, ye shall receive. (Matt. 21:22)

I prayed for comfort, and God gave it to me. I wasn't surprised; God answered every single prayer I prayed during that week in the hospital. Seriously, every little thing I asked for, He gave me. I would be cold, and I would pray for warmth. I received it. I would be scared, and I would pray for wisdom. I received it. He never forgot me. When I needed strength, I prayed and received it. From the tiniest little wish to the most extreme request, God made it happen.

Have you every prayed for something that you didn't receive? I have plenty of times, and it is hard to comprehend sometimes. We can pray with the best of intentions, but if we aren't praying for God's will, we are praying for the wrong thing.

> Ye ask, and receive not, because ye ask
> amiss, that ye may consume it upon your lusts.
> (James 4:3)

We don't know the entire story; we only know the part of the story that affects us. His plan is much greater than we can comprehend. It is easy to be selfish and ask for our individual wants, but if it doesn't serve His plan, we are doing ourselves a disservice. I trust in Him. He made all and knows all, and He loves us. I believe His plan has only the best intentions for the church of Jesus Christ. As long as you're a member of His church, you will have a peace and appreciation for our Father's plan.

In my prayers during that time and now still, I always included that ultimately, I wanted His will to be done. If it meant that I would receive my wishes, then so be it; but if not, I understood. After all, I was at His mercy. I had submitted myself to His will throughout all of this, and I wasn't about to stop.

Right before we went to sleep, Jerry wanted a snack. I had quite the accumulation of snacks in my pile of belongings, and I rifled through it to find an apple. It was an Organic Gala Apple that I had purchased on that past Friday. Our daughter loves apples. I held the apple up and told him how I had bought it for her, but since she wasn't at home to eat it, I had brought it with me so it wouldn't go to waste sitting at home. He usually prefers salty and savory snacks, but he shrugged his shoulders and took the apple. Then he requested a knife to slice it with.

Possibly from lack of proper rest or maybe from lack of nutrition, my mind made the decision to hand him a large pocketknife. The knife had belonged to my grandfather. He wanted to give it to Jerry but passed away before he had the chance. My grandmother recently found it and gave it to me to take home to Jerry the day prior to his near-fatal emergency. It was still in my purse, and without giving it a second thought, I handed it to Jerry and told him the story. My husband, who could barely feed himself from being so weak, now had a large pocketknife in his hands!

He so clumsily sliced the apple, as I feared that he would slice a finger right off! Jerry would take a bite and lay the open knife on a pillow balanced on his belly. The knife would wobble back and forth and even fell blade-first onto his leg at one point! Just then, Jerry's nurse for that night walked in the room. I could tell he was nervous to see his patient with that knife. He was trying to administer Jerry's medications, but the open knife was making him nervous. His nurse grabbed the knife like it was a loaded gun and carefully sat it over on the table as he said in such a funny voice, "I'm just going to move your weapon over here for a minute."

Inside, I was laughing so hard! My husband chuckled and said that he was trying to eat his "generic" apple. We were all quiet for a second and then the nurse asked, "What's a generic apple?"

Jerry had confused the word "organic" with "generic," and we all laughed about what a generic apple could be. God has a good sense of humor, and I needed a good laugh to decompress from the stress of everything. We still laugh about that today.

I prayed for both of us to rest well that night, and we did.

That was Wednesday.

Thursday morning came quick. We both woke up refreshed and ready for an exciting day! We were being blessed with a pacemaker/defibrillator. Hallelujah! The electrical team came early and took Jerry back for his procedure. The implantation went flawlessly, and his team of doctors agreed that he would most likely go home the next day. Dr. Brunson came by for a visit. He had worked for six days straight, every single day that we had been at the hospital, and he was ready for a day off. He told us that we all had witnessed a miracle. In his twenty-five years of practicing medicine, Dr. Brunson had never had a patient fully recover from ventricular fibrillation and been able to walk out of the hospital. He marveled at Jerry one more time, and we said our goodbyes. I adore Dr. Brunson!

During our stay in the NICU and the first step-down unit, children were not allowed to visit. I guess there was one perk of our stay in the basic hospital room—our daughter could now visit us! My dad brought her in for a visit. We hadn't seen her in six days! Oh my goodness, how I missed that girl. She was a bit shy during the visit. I think seeing her daddy in that hospital bed scared her. Other than being born in one, she had never seen a hospital. It was all new for her, but she sure was glad to be in her mommy's arms! She didn't want to leave me at the end of the visit. She bawled her eyes out as I told her goodbye at the elevators. I didn't want to send her back for another night at my dad's house, even though she would get spoiled rotten at Pappy and Grammy's, but I couldn't leave my husband's side. I had to stay with him. They left, and my heart broke for her. I swore to her that this would be our last night away from home.

I went home for a few hours to clean up the living room. I didn't want Jerry to come home and see everything disheveled from the chaos that occurred nearly a week ago. There were muddy footprints all over the entryway and living room. His dinner plate was lying on our daughter's beanbag chair. I had spilled his nitro pills in an effort to get a single one to place in his mouth. The furniture was awry, and the atmosphere in the house was somber. I cleaned and arranged and ran essential oil diffusers in every room. I finished tidying up and then took a shower. That had to be the best shower of my life! Then I put on clean clothes, packed Jerry a bag of toiletries and clean clothes for the ride home, and headed back to the hospital for one more night. I should mention that I forgot to pack his shoes. Bless him.

We had a very special dinner delivery that night. Jerry's soon-to-be son-in-law was the executive chef at a very nice restaurant downtown. He brought us a delicious meal of filet mignon, pork chops, short ribs, and all kinds of scrumptious sides. That was a real treat for all of us! After nearly a week of not eating and then eating hospital food, the upscale dinner was such a treat for both of us! Jerry's sister dined with us in that dingy hospital room. There we were, using linen napkins and eating off of real dishes with real silverware. We were just missing candles and music! That meal is a great memory for me; it was quite a celebration!

That was Thursday.

On Friday we waited and waited, and then we waited some more. We assumed that we would be going home, but the nurses knew nothing of it. The day before, the doctors had all agreed that we could go home on Friday, yet we waited all morning and afternoon for the official word that we could leave.

While we waited, I wrote thank-you cards for the nurses Jerry had in the NICU and delivered them with cookies. I was thrilled when Jason, our nurse from Sunday, walked over to see us and thank us for his card. Jason has the best smile, and it thrilled me to see the joy on his face as he spoke with my husband. I knew that Jason was proud of my husband's progress, although he wouldn't let it show. Jason was humble and wouldn't take any credit. I think he knew that it was all God's handiwork. I told Jason that God had worked through him and the entire medical team. He agreed.

Also, during our time waiting to go home, my mind raced with excitement because not only had God given me a story to tell, but He had also inspired me to write it all in a book (this book)! I felt like one of the wisehearted women from Exodus weaving goat's hair, except instead of goat's hair, I would be using words to craft my special project! I've never written a book, but I love writing. So just how can I properly execute God's mission? For starters, I was willing; but also, He gave me the tools I needed. He was instilling gifts to my heart right then and there!

I've used writing as a creative outlet for years, but I've never shared it publicly. In school, writing papers was my favorite! Others would cringe, but I could knock out a paper easily. God had actually laid it on my heart back at the Thanksgiving prior to these events to write a book, but I thought that the subject would be much different. That particular subject is still on my heart to share, but after witnessing this miraculous event, God clearly told me that my first book would be used to spread this story. My ears and heart were open to His message, and I was glad to use my gifts for His glory.

Use Your Gifts in What You Do

My gift is different than your gift
And my message is different than yours too
God so wondrously created us differently
To use our gifts in everything we do

Don't miss the message
It's exclusively for you
Don't miss the message
Use your gifts in what you do

You were made for this, not that
I was made for this, where I'm at
We are not the same, but we are equal in value
We are unique, so use your gifts in what you do

Don't miss the message
It's exclusively for you
Don't miss the message
Use your gifts in what you do

Finally, the moment we had been waiting for—we were going home! Seven days prior, almost to the hour, Jerry was being rushed to the hospital via ambulance. The flooding rains that fell upon us seven days ago had finally cleared, and Jerry rode home healthy under calm skies. Nearly 168 hours ago, we had no idea what the following week would entail. God was there through it all, vibrantly revealing Himself to us with all of His glory!

I was excited and nervous for Jerry to come home. I felt as though the victim was nervously returning to the scene of the crime. I worried that I wouldn't be able to care for him properly. He was a fall risk. His short-term memory was still lacking. Along with caring for him, I would also be caring for our daughter. I knew it would be tough, but the Holy Spirit would be with me, and God's blessings would still pour down on us all.

That night, I struggled to get Jerry comfortable. He couldn't lay flat on our bed, and he couldn't get comfortable in the recliner. The poor thing slept sitting up on the couch. I checked on him a few times throughout the night. Sometimes he would be sleeping, and sometimes he would be sitting there awake. Our daughter and I cuddled without him in our big king-sized bed, but we were all under one roof again, and that was special.

That was Friday.

Seven days had passed. Those seven days contained every emotion possible. From the shock of an unexpected devastation to the joy of having a second chance with the love of my life, God was with me the entire way. I was exhausted, but where there's a will, there's a way.

I dedicated myself to helping my husband regain his full quality of life. We took his recovery day by day and sometimes hour by hour. The strongest man I've ever known couldn't even walk through the house unassisted. We headed down a long road of recovery. It started with regaining strength in both mind and body. I worked diligently to prepare nutritious meals for him. I dug deep and found patience I never knew I had. Caring for both him and our daughter proved to be trying at times, but we put our nose to the grindstone and got it done.

After over forty years of smoking a pack a day, Jerry quit. He hadn't lit up since before his drive home from work seven days ago. Why should he start now? He had one week under his belt, and even though he was unconscious for *three* days of that week, it was quite an accomplishment. His mind was exasperated from the lack of short-term memory, and the nicotine withdrawals compounded the frustration. I mentioned that Jerry is the strongest man I've ever known, but I should also say that he is the most patient person I've ever known too. This man exudes the patience of Job, but during his recovery, his fuse was noticeably shorter. He's the one who usually has enough patience for the both of us. During recovery, I had more than he did, and that's not very much.

He still wasn't resting well. We bought an adjustable bed, thinking that he would be able to get comfortable, but he still couldn't sleep in bed. He spent every night for weeks sleeping upright on the couch.

Springtime comes early in East Tennessee. Even in the winter, we can have spring-like days. As we were recovering at home, winter was turning into spring, and I found refuge in spending time outside. Oftentimes, the temperatures would be too cold for Jerry and our daughter, so I would escape outside by myself for some alone time. My body would be working hard, but my mind would be relaxing. I focused on raking leaves or cleaning out flower beds, and it eased my mind of the stress it had been baffled with. I recalled details of my experiences both in the hospital and with my angelic encounter before and brainstormed on how I would patch together the pieces of my story for this book. I was developing the mental capacity for this project. The therapy was incomparable with anything I could have received elsewhere. Thank you, God, for the beauty of creation.

Praise to Above

I would take my last drink of water and give it to a rose
So as I lay there dying, I could watch it grow
Then I'll slip off to my Savior in a place more divine
And leave at peace with the love that I left behind

To God be the glory; He made everything
To God be the glory; just look and hear Him sing
Through the beauty of a blooming rose, He sends off songs of love
To God be the glory; praise to above

I would share my last bite of food with a bird too weak to fly
So I could watch him soar as my soul flies high
Then I'll slip off to my Savior in a place more divine
And leave at peace with the love that I left behind

To God be the glory; He made everything
To God be the glory; just look and hear Him sing
Through the beauty of a soaring bird, He sends off songs of love
To God be the glory; praise to above

A summer storm, a babbling stream, the cool shade from a tall oak tree
A purring kitten, falling snow, warm sand beneath my toes
Butterflies and thunderous herds, reading the Living Word
Through the beauty of creation, He sends us songs of love
To God be the glory; praise to above

I fell in love with God's creation during this time! East Tennessee, in my opinion, is one of the most beautiful places under God's creation. I'm surrounded by the beauty of the Great Smoky Mountains every day, and I've never taken it for granted. The hills and views and spectacular sunsets are really a sight! We're surrounded by breathtaking farms, lakes, wooded areas, and wildlife. Even with all of this beauty, I've never been so taken with creation like I was that spring in my very own yard. With my hands in the dirt and my lungs filled with the fresh spring air, new life was breathed into me. Daffodils sprang up like bright, cheerful smiles. The birds sang to me. The dead winter foliage transformed into gorgeous greenery, and my whole world seemed to sing.

Overall, the first month of Jerry's recovery was long and slow. He was committed to gaining the strength in his body and mind. Every day he pushed himself a bit more. He had to put up with my nagging to drink enough water, cut back on the soda, eat enough fruits and vegetables, and so on. He did a great job, and our hard work was paying off. The progress in the first month was certainly slow, but our optimism was growing.

In month two of his recovery, he began to do mild yard work with me outside and light household chores. He was still not cleared to drive, so I would drive him everywhere. I thought it was fun, but I'm not so sure he would agree! He basically had zero time to himself, but I enjoyed soaking up every single moment with him. It was a bonding experience that we had never had before. We laughed and talked and grew closer together. We had the time together both as a couple and a family, which we wouldn't have been able have to if our schedules would have been normal. You know how life gets in the way of life. We're all busy and often overworked. We can get preoccupied mentally, which doesn't allow us to be fully present with our loved ones, even when we are physically there. Neither of us was working. We weren't preoccupied with other responsibilities. Our only responsibilities were to each other, and it was a beautiful time in our lives.

All of his follow-up appointments went better than expected, and his entire team of doctors agreed that his case was exceptional. We were in the month of April, and spring was in full bloom. So was our optimism. We live in an old farmhouse, and our property is filled with mature landscape. Our yard features a wide variety of flowering plants and shrubs, and springtime is when it looks the best. I think that, that particular spring was the best we'd ever seen. Perhaps it was because our eyes appreciated it more, but I saw beauty in places I had never seen it before.

We never thought that Jerry would go back to work. He thoroughly enjoyed what he did for a living. Jerry worked outside every day on a farm. The fresh air and the exercise were good for him, and the level of stress with his job was basically zero. He had been off work for two months, and we were trying to figure out what our financial future looked like. We hoped that he would be able to return, but we feared that he would need to find a job with less physical requirements. I cannot express enough how wonderful his employer was during Jerry's recovery. They were beyond patient and accommodating during Jerry's recovery. They understood the fact that even though Jerry wanted to come back to work, we weren't sure if that was an option.

In the third month, Jerry's recovery began to progress quickly. He was now taking on larger projects in our yard. His vigor was back, and his mind was able to remember short-term details much more clearly. I was impressed, and I thought he was surprising himself too! We had disability papers in hand during one doctor's visit because we thought Jerry would not be able to return to work, but his cardiologist advised him that at his age, going back to work would be the best option for him. He stated that so many times, he saw patients give up after a medical event like this, and then their health declined rapidly. He felt that Jerry was capable of regaining his lifestyle by 100 percent and that he felt it was safe for Jerry to go back to work. After a few weeks of cardiac rehab, Jerry was cleared to go back to work!

Three months after nearly losing his life, he went back to work. The man who was on his deathbed was back at it, weed-eating and running chainsaws and working on the farm. He was exerting himself physically, and I knew it was good for his body and mind.

I felt like I was sending my child off to their first day of school. Once he started going to work again, I missed him! Having those *three* months with him was a blessing, but having my husband healthy enough to go back to work was an even greater blessing.

Life returned to normal, and now it seems almost like it never even happened.

Nursing my husband back to health was the greatest honor I've had in my life. It wasn't easy, especially while also caring for our daughter, but I cherished every moment. Sometimes I was brought to tears, and sometimes we were able to laugh. But in all times, we praised God. I would do it all over again, and I'd do it for the rest of my life if that's what he needed. Just to have more time with him was blessing enough for me, but to see him eventually make a full recovery has my heart bursting with gratitude!

When I think back on it all, it seems too crazy to be true. Sometimes I would wonder, did all of that really happen? It felt like I had been living in a whirlwind, but even so, the lessons I learned from it all are still with me. I'm not just talking about what I learned during our time at the hospital and during Jerry's recovery period. God had been grooming me for *three* months leading up to the moment when I almost lost my husband. Because of what I learned in those *three* months, I was prepared and ready for the adversity I would face on that February 22. My heart was being stirred up, and God was strategically giving me the gifts I would need.

SECTION 3

Thankfully, There Was a
Stirring-Up in Me

Let's go back in time, *three* months from that scary February 22. I've mentioned how God had been preparing me for what lay ahead, and it is ironic that He would spark my journey on Thanksgiving Day.

Thanksgiving Day of 2018 was on November 22, and on that day God inspired me to immerse myself into the Living Word. I never imagined that exactly *three* months later, I would be clinging to my faith during the lowest point in my life.

Our daughter was sick that day, and we missed out on our planned Thanksgiving celebration. We stayed home and threw together a last-minute meal of our own. After indulging in our minifeast and a post-meal nap, I was thinking forward to the Christmas season. Usually on Thanksgiving night, I would unpack our Christmas decorations and begin putting up our tree, but this particular year I had already decorated our home for Christmas weeks prior. I sat on our couch, looking around our sparkling room, thinking what's next for this Christmas season.

God whispered to my heart, and my eyes opened wide. What better way to celebrate our Lord's birth than by reading the Gospels? Duh! Why didn't I think of that? It happened so fast. I had just asked the question to myself, and immediately He gave me the answer. His voice was crystal clear.

Just being honest here, I had never read the Gospels all the way through. I've read chapters and studied those red letters, but I had never studied all four Gospels together in their entirety. That night I began reading the book of Matthew. Every single night, as we slipped into bed, I would open the Bible Jerry had gifted me years ago, and I would read. It was exactly what my soul needed.

Just the simple act of opening my Bible and reading a few chapters got me feeling closer to my Lord. My heart absorbed the story of our Savior, and my eyes focused intently on those red letters. My soul became thirsty for more.

The Living Word is mysterious. I'm sure you'll agree that every time you read a chapter again, you pick up on something new and different from the time before. God speaks to us through His Word, and He allows our minds to comprehend exactly what we need at that given time. At that point, God was opening my heart and mind for the message I needed to hear. This message would fuel my soul in preparation for the coming months. He was imparting wisdom unto me to stop wasting my time in actions that did not allow me to grow spiritually and to start living a more Christlike life.

It began with reading the Bible every day. I started with Matthew and finished John by Christmas. It was one of the best experiences of my life! As I dived further into the Bible, my focus on the Lord grew, and my time spent on meaningless things waned. I was sacrificing time spent either scrolling on my phone or watching the television to spend more time with God's Word. I spent less time in the world's noise and more time in the quietness of my home. Doing so allowed my mind to pause. I was resting and gaining spiritual strength.

By focusing on the Gospels and our Lord during His birth and His short life, my Christmas season was personally more meaningful and less stressful. During the holidays, we sing about things like peace, being merry, embracing traditions, and the celebration of our Savior's birth; but our actions paint a different picture. I, for one, run myself ragged buying, decorating, and attending; but in 2018 I enjoyed a simple, cozy Christmas.

Also, on that Thanksgiving Day, I decided to stop watching the news. I had been a news junkie for years. God laid it on my heart to quit cold turkey! I thought about it, and I had been watching an average of eight hours of news per day. That's crazy, y'all! Who does that?

Are you as crazy as I was? Flipping the news on was the first thing I did each morning. I would watch it for a few hours while I drank coffee and had breakfast, and then I would keep it on in the background while I piddled around the house. This would last until the noon news went off, and then I would turn it back on at four in the afternoon. On top of that, in certain times of the year, we would watch well into the evening. I couldn't get enough election or hurricane coverage. When it came to local news, I could practically recite the stories, as they were repeated throughout the day. Oh, and cable news was a thrill! The banter and opinions and bias, bias, bias. I didn't realize how suffocating it was until God opened my eyes!

Scripture warns us of what's to come as the end of time nears, and I had a front-row seat to the coverage. It is difficult to comprehend the atrocities that are occurring in our world. I don't want to come across as unconcerned or inconsiderate, and I do believe that we need to know what's going on; but at some point, I had to realize that I can only worry about what I can change. The same stories, the same drama, and the same bias were splattered all over the atmosphere of my home; and I hated it. The stories would weigh me down; and instead of praying for this world, I would allow the stories to tear me down, infuriate me, and cloud my focus. Suddenly, I realized that the best way for me to make a difference in this world was to begin at home.

I have no plans to enter politics. Do you? I can't battle the terrorists or fix the border crisis, but I can teach my daughter to love Jesus. I can't handpick our politicians, but I can visit the polls as an informed voter without spending eight hours of my day drenching myself in the filth of an election. It's okay to stay updated; but like everything else, moderation is important, and we cannot allow anything to shift focus for what is truly important: a relationship with Jesus. With so much time spent on the news and other things, I wasn't capable of giving myself fully to the Lord or accepting His gifts.

The greatest gift God has ever given me is the chance of being a wife and a mother. Not only has He given me the opportunity, but

He has given me a willing heart to grow and learn to become better and better in my role.

How can we set our priority on the positivity of God's plan if we are spending so much time absorbing the negativity of Satan's actions? God's plan for me at this point in my life is to be a devoted wife and mother, to grow spiritually, and to form the roots I'll need to branch out into my future. I don't know exactly what my future holds, but you can bet I'll be doing something for the will of God! Whatever it will be, I'm strengthening my foundation now. My entire life has been a building process. All my sins and past experiences have been nourishment for my growth. During this time of spiritual growth, I was a glutton for God's Word and direction. I wanted truth and clarity! A strong foundation cannot be built upon falseness.

Just like that, the news and its negativity were out of my life! I have my opinions, and I'm entitled to that. But I'm done following the details of every godless story. If more people were following the Lord, the news organizations would have much less to cover. Or better yet, we would be watching stories of heartwarming inspiration that would celebrate our daily God-honoring actions. The coverage available to us now is rarely about the good in this world. We're watching it, and our own lives are influenced. I want to dive deep into what God wants, and I believe that God wants me to grow in my faith and spread the love of Jesus Christ. *That's* the influence that this world needs. It's as simple as that. Following the failures of humanity is not where I'm supposed to be. I'm supposed to be following the Lord!

Without the weight of a full day of news coverage, I instantly felt lighter. I was happier. The impact was immediate, but I didn't stop there.

Like Adam and Eve suddenly realizing that they were naked, I realized that I was dirty. Filth had been leaking into my mind from all directions. From my phone to my television, Satan was intruding on me and my family, and he was using our screens and the media to do it.

I went through my social media accounts and unfollowed most news organizations and pages that didn't contribute to my newfound quest for positivity. I blocked some people; it had to be done. I learned that sharing a news story or posting my opinion wasn't going to change the world. Would you change your opinion on "Insert Topic Here" after reading one of my rants? No. Am I going to change my opinion after reading your post? No! I don't want to see yours, and you don't want to see mine. I have my opinions, and you have yours, and arguing over social media doesn't fix anything. Switching my moral authority on God's Word instead of our political climate was like a breath of fresh air, and just like that, the drama disappeared. I'm glad I've learned this, and I can move on from the wrath of social media debates.

I have friends and family with all kinds of views. My goal is to be as respectful as possible and to pray. I pray that I make the correct decisions. I pray that my loved ones will too, and it is important to pray for our leaders. No matter what party they belong to, just pray. God will take care of the rest.

Even after cleaning up my accounts, I took it a step further and quit looking at social media for a while. I would go days and sometimes weeks without opening those apps on my phone. Have you ever taken a social media break? If so, then you know how rewarding it can be. Sadly, we live in a world where we've lost touch with our loved ones. With so many different ways to communicate now, it's ironic that the quality of communication has declined. I go months without seeing my friends in real life, and I wish we spent more time together. Now, all I know about their lives is what I see online. Perhaps if we all totally ditched the digital realm, we would make space for making real-life memories together.

I wish we could go back in time and sit on each other's porches and entertain our loved ones with meals and glasses of iced tea and good ole-fashioned conversation. I long for connection like our ancestors had.

Every now and then, I'll scroll through the social media feeds and see what's going on; but it takes a lot of energy out of me, and I don't like that. Negativity always finds a way to slip in, and I've become very strict on what I allow into my life.

I rarely post anything to certain social realms. Does anyone even miss my online presence? I don't think so.

As a stay-at-home mom, I spend most of my time at home. The TV was always on. Whether or not I was watching it, it was on in the background. My daughter doesn't watch TV. It doesn't keep her attention, and I'm glad. The television being on all day was for me, and once I realized what I was allowing into our home, I shut it off. Even though she wasn't watching it, I know that some of it was being absorbed into her innocent and precious brain.

Do we still watch TV? Yes, and probably still too much of it. The language and content on most networks are shocking to me. I was allowing that filth into my home. Looking for the quickest way to clean your home? The power button on your remote is a great place to start.

I have witnessed firsthand how the influence of seemingly harmless media can influence decision-making. As a teenager, one of my favorite shows led me to believe that being promiscuous was cool and exciting. Seriously, a television show planted the seed in my mind that sex outside of marriage and at a young age was perfectly fine. The devil was on my shoulder whispering sweet nothings into my ear, but there was nothing on my other shoulder talking me back from the cliff. I wasn't listening to God. I hadn't studied Scripture to feel convicted during the decision-making, and nobody in my life knew what was going on in my mind. With the devil as my guide, I jumped into a world of desire. Now, I look back on my actions, and I cringe at what I was doing with my life. I don't need those same influences affecting my daughter.

I realize that the way is narrow, and I'm willing to sacrifice this worldly influence for a much easier walk down the *free*way. Jesus Christ clearly laid it all out for us, but it's easy to get lost when the devil is driving. Jesus's road is straight and narrow as we know it, but I feel much lighter walking in the light. The masses are singing songs of sin and celebrating it. On the *free*way, I don't miss any of it. Rather, I'm delighted by a newfound freedom, and with each step I feel lighter. After these simple changes, I saw everything in this world differently. As trivial as it sounds, certain songs, television shows, and movies struck a different chord in my heart; and I realized what I was allowing into my life.

This new awakening opened my eyes to the music I was listening to. I love music, but I no longer found delight in the songs I had been singing. As a teenager, I rapped along with lyrics that celebrated violence and degraded women. I hummed along with songs that were so outrageous that I didn't even understand what the words meant. When the message is delivered by someone with charisma and a catchy beat, we'll sing along to anything! Do you want your children reciting lyrics that rejoice at and encourage sin? I sure don't.

> He that tilleth his land shall be satisfied
> with bread; but he that followeth vain persons is
> void of understanding. (Prov. 12:11)

The entertainment industry has too much control over our lives, but their power doesn't exist if they don't have our attention. It's time to turn off the dirt. Not all of it is bad, I must say, but I feel as though a majority of what we're being entertained by does not make God smile.

We should be praying for our leaders, all of them. Usually, that means the leaders of our government (regardless of their party affiliation), but it really should also include those who appear as leaders. Our nation's youth and even many adults are looking up to celebrities, so let's pray for them too. Let's pray for all leaders so they'll focus on honoring God, finding conviction in their hearts, and for them to accept Jesus as their Savior.

In the book of Jude, we are warned of false teachers. They existed two thousand years ago, and more than ever, we have them today too.

> These are murmurers, complainers, walking
> after their own lusts; and their mouth speaketh
> great swelling words, flattering people to gain
> advantage. (Jude 1:16)

We are sinners. We lust after worldly pleasures because it is easy. Sometimes we naturally fall into the devil's hand because we seek what we want to find. We might not like what God has to say on a particular subject, so we defiantly twist Scripture or deny it completely until we convince ourselves that something is okay. After that, we convince others too. We search from source to source until we find someone who can deliver the message we want to hear because it makes us feel better about ourselves. We turn our backs on Scripture and make our own rules. This is wrong, and because of false teachings (wherever they come from), many of us will spend eternity in hell.

Sounds dramatic, doesn't it? And a little over the top? Well, it's the truth.

Only God knows everything. I don't know enough to be making my own way though this world. I have to trust in God's plan and follow His Word. What a relief that I don't have to make such big decisions anymore. I simply look to see what His word says, and then I can run and hide behind it. When you feel like the world is closing in on you because of your beliefs, hide behind His Word, and He will shield you from the devil's wrath.

All of humanity, our neighbors, friends, family, brothers and sisters, and especially our children are learning from the sights and sounds of this world. Instead of speaking facts on God's Word and the actual teachings of Jesus Christ, there are those who have "crept in unawares" and are corrupting the truth. We are allowing these teachings into our homes. Whether you and your family are learning from a false pastor, a politician, an entertainer, or even a loved one who is unknowingly sharing false doctrines with you, *you* are the gatekeeper to your eternal life; and you must determine which information is true or false.

What is your authority?

Is it your friend? Is it what you see on television? Is it what our current president said or maybe what the past president said? Is it the new hit song or the hilarious movie that just came out? Is it the interview with a celebrity you read in a magazine? Is it your coworker, your mother, the news anchor, or maybe you don't even have one? Our authority should be God and God alone. Our authority should be found within the Living Word. I am not wise enough to be anyone's authority; likewise, no man is wise enough to be mine.

I love the poetic way that Jude describes false teachers:

> These are stains in your feasts of love, when they feast with you, feeding themselves without fear: clouds they are without water, carried about of winds: trees whose fruit withereth, without fruit, twice dead, plucked up by the roots;
>
> Raging waves of the sea, foaming out of their own shame; wandering stars, to whom is reserved the blackness of darkness for ever. (Jude 1:12–13)

Back to how I've been cleaning up my life, I started to look at how much time and money I spent on materialism. My house was busting at the seams with stuff. I began to pack it up and get it out—donate it, sell it, repurpose if possible, or throw it away. We were drowning in a sea of merchandise here in our household, and I was the culprit! I was the absolute worst at this. My largest pitfall was stuff. Shopping is fun, especially at flea markets and garage sales. I love to hunt for treasures, and I love sales! Having so much stuff is like carrying around emotional baggage! It's heavy and consuming. Giving up news and social media was easy. Materialism was much harder for me. It still defeats me every day.

Remember the selfish and immature me that I described in the first section of this book? Before I was saved, I was addicted to accomplishments. I went through a period in my life when I had to achieve goals to feel good about myself. I guess there could be worse ways of reaching toward self-satisfaction, but I put 100 percent of my energy into earthly accomplishments and 0 percent into God. From running a full marathon to receiving my bachelor's degree, I made a list of goals and checked them off one by one and sometimes two by two. I couldn't be stopped; I was literally addicted to achievements.

> I made me great works; I builded me houses;
> I planted me vineyards:
> I made me gardens and orchards, and I
> planted trees in them of all kind of fruits:
> I made me pools of water, to water there-
> with the wood that bringeth forth trees:
> I got me servants and maidens, and had ser-
> vants born in my house; also I had great posses-
> sions of great and small cattle above all that were
> in Jerusalem before me:
> I gathered me also silver and gold, and the
> peculiar treasure of kings and of the provinces:
> I acquired me men singers and women singers,
> and the delights of the sons of men, as musical
> instruments, and that of all sorts.
> So I was great, and increased more than all
> that were before me in Jerusalem: also my wis-
> dom remained within me.
> And whatsoever mine eyes desired I kept not
> from them, I withheld not my heart from any joy;
> for my heart rejoiced in all my labor: and this was
> my reward of all my labor. (Eccles. 2:4–10)

Those are not my words. Those are the words of King Solomon, but they sum up the self-pride that I had worked so diligently for. I had everything I ever wanted. I never said no to myself. I needed my things and my achievements so I could have the identity I wanted. My identity stood between me and God. During this awakening, I looked back on my life and was disappointed that I had wasted so much time and effort on achievements that didn't truly matter. I'd like to say that some of it were for the glory of God, but in reality it was all for me.

Then I looked on all the works that my hands had wrought, and on the labor that I had labored to do: and, behold, all was vanity and a grasping for the wind, and there was no profit under the sun. (Eccles. 2:11)

I am not saying that we shouldn't set personal goals, that we shouldn't have interests, and that we shouldn't work to be good at what we do. I also don't what anyone to think that I'm an advocate for being lazy. God gave us unique gifts and abilities, and we must be responsible for how we use them. What I am saying is that I placed all my efforts into my own personal accomplishments when really I should have been working to glorify God and not myself. After all, there is no profit under this sun. Our gain is in heaven.

Are you a cloud without water carried about by winds? Or are you grasping for the wind in vain? I have been guilty of both.

Leavin' Even

Just as we came in, we leave this world without
You can spend your life buying, but there's no doubt
We're leavin' even

Toss your jewelry out the window and your money down the drain
As for your accomplishments, you can do the same
'Cause we're leavin' even; we're leavin' even

We are leavin' even, but what have you done today
To build up your treasures and stow them all away
Because the Lord is preparing for us; He will call us from the skies
We will enter heaven even and then receive our prize

We're leavin' even; we're leavin' even

Your neighborhoods and cars, they won't get you far

He will come and find you wherever you are
'Cause we're leavin' even; we're leavin' even

We are leavin' even, but what have you done today
To build up your treasures and stow them all away
Because the Lord is preparing for us; He will call us from the skies
We will enter heaven even and then receive our prize

We're leavin' even; we're leavin' even

The devil uses many methods to fuel his endeavor. He's going down (literally), and he desires to take as many of us as possible with him. He knows how the story ends, yet still he fights and fights. You and I are nothing but casualties in the devil's eyes, but as soldiers in God's army, it is our responsibility to spread the truth and the word of eternal salvation through Christ. This is how we can fight! With Christ, we win. Without Christ, the devil wins. Whose side are you on?

I believe that during these times, there is a natural void in every person's life, and it is up to the individual to fill it. God gives us the choice as to what we fill it with. Since the moment Adam and Eve gave into temptation, our perfectness has been nonexistent, and we long to fill the emptiness we struggle with. We're being hypnotized with false teachings, entertainment, and materialism. It's easy to fill the void with those things, but nothing can truly fulfill someone's life like walking with the Holy Spirit. Anything that takes up valuable space in our lives and comes before Jesus needs to be reconsidered. Are our thoughts and actions honoring Him? God gives us the choice, and I am beyond blessed to have the knowledge to choose Him. Even though it is a daily battle, I fight to fill my void with more God.

By eliminating a large portion of falseness from my life, I've allowed more space for God. This has made me hungry for more, and I am constantly striving to further clean my mind, heart, and home. Eliminating the junk is a work in progress for me, and given the enormity of junk in this world, it probably will always be.

I'm up here on this soapbox because God has a plan for all of us, and it does not include wasting our short lives on anything that don't honor Him. I'm a sinner, yes, but I am cleansed again and again. God knows my heart, and He knows my struggles. Over and over again, I fail or fall short. Over and over again, God loves me unconditionally. The same goes for you too.

To Clear the Clutter of This World

By now, you might be thinking that I've fallen off my rocker. Do you think I sound like a grumpy old man? I'm starting to think those grumpy old men are onto something! But seriously, what I am trying to do here is encourage you to take a look at your life and decide whether or not you're on the right path. For me, I needed to clean up my life to get on the right track. God has a big plan for me, and I'm eager to fulfill His will. I believe we all have clutter in our lives, and if we place some effort into eliminating it, our world will become a better place. That has got to be the best way to make a difference in your home, local community and, consequently, the entire world!

What can you achieve by clearing your clutter?

God inspired me to close the door on my clutter and open the new one He placed in front of me. I'm afraid of what my life would be like now if I hadn't listened to Him.

By making efforts to clean up my life, I made room for the things that really mattered. Without the worthless noise of the news, television, and social media, I could hear God talking to me. I had been spending my time on tasks that didn't glorify God in the way I wanted to worship him. After taking the initial steps to clean my life, God was directing me to be a better wife and a more present mother. The TV and the internet, among other things, were holding me back from properly fulfilling those duties, and while I'm not winning awards for wife or mother of the year, I am conscious of my actions and actively reaching toward being a better woman.

Do you spend more time staring at your phone and less time focusing on the loved ones right in front of you? It's easy to do, and it's quite the distraction. By giving up or reducing such temptations, I began to be more present for my family.

My husband and my daughter are the two most important people in my life, and how many hours did I lose with them because I was scrolling? How many hours did I waste on the screens of my phone, computer, and television when I could have been studying my Bible? I feel like I've wasted years of my life!

I almost lost my husband. I would have spent the rest of this life regretting the time I missed with him and the time wasted on meaningless things. Our time on this earth is short and valuable, and I learned that the hard way.

God sparked an incredible fire within my soul, and in those *three* months, I found myself. I grew up quicker in those *three* months than I had done in the past thirty years.

Change Me, Use Me

Only One is perfect
As for the rest of us, we are flawed
Without the love of the perfect Son
There's no healing for our scars

Change me like You changed Saul
Use me like You used Paul
Scars are on us all
Oh, scars are on us all

Of all the sins I have committed
They've all been washed away
Without those scars I wouldn't have
My story to share today

Change me like You changed Saul
Use me like You used Paul
Scars are on us all
Oh, scars are on us all

So there I was, struck by the glory
I'll never know why He chose me
Why me? I am not worthy
Worthy is the Lamb

Thanksgiving Day has a new meaning for me. It's as special as the day I was saved. That November 22 was the day of my spiritual awakening and rebirth. I consider November 22 to be another birthday for me!

I don't believe I would have had the strength to handle the trials of nearly losing my husband like I did if I had been weighed down by the devil's negativity. After making major changes in my daily routine, I was brought out of my lowliness and raised beyond measure.

I was able to save my husband's life because He saved me.

Now with my spiritual strength and willingness to obey God, I am on a mission. My mission starts here with sharing this story. I'm not sure exactly what my full mission entails. I know God will reveal an awesome plan for me, and whatever it is, I will obey. I'm excited to see what my future holds! I honestly believe I can do anything, and most importantly, I can do it to glorify Him.

I want to know what you can accomplish with the help of the Holy Spirit. What is your mission? How are you going to spend your short time here on earth? I'm still searching for all the gifts God had given me. What are your gifts? Are you using them?

What can you do because He saved you?

I can do all things through Christ which strengtheneth me. (Phil. 4:13)

With Christ, all things are possible. Look at the achievements in your life. I look back at mine before I held the hand of the Holy Spirit, and they are all meaningless in the scope of what this life is all about. God gave us a fun and beautiful world to live this life in, but if your hobbies and interests interfere with your relationship with Him, it's time to examine how you're spending your time. In my past, I worked hard to achieve goals I had set for myself. Sure, I had fun, but I was dedicating 100 percent of my time working for myself and my own desires. If I had spent a small portion of that effort on helping others, my community would be that much brighter. I've made changes in my life, and I'm working for God now!

He provides for me. He guides me. He comforts me and has given me a blessed life. I enjoy the beautiful world we live in. I still enjoy my hobbies, but I don't place priority on them like I did in the past. Instead, I make time for Him first. My faith is my priority, and although I still sometimes find myself stepping back into my old routine, He gives me the self-awareness to get back on track.

My faith came full circle throughout all of this. Jerry led me to the Lord, and as I was saved, I received the Holy Spirit. Then as a saved child of God, I opened my heart and cleared my mind to receive His messages. During my spiritual awakening, I set my sights on glorifying Him. He strengthened me, and through His strength I saved my husband's earthly life. Now, with this story, I am on a mission to give God the glory He deserves!

Ultimately, it wasn't my husband's time to depart from this world. God has a big plan for him. Recently, I heard my daughter giggling along with her daddy while playing in the next room. Sometimes I can get too caught up in being serious. I'm goal-driven, and I like to stay on track. My husband is much better at embracing the moment and being silly. It is moments like that when I'm thankful that she has both of us. The early loss of my husband would have changed everything for my daughter's future. I want her to have each of our attributes to blend together with beauty, and we both work on instilling a love of God within her.

We've got to ask ourselves some serious questions. Life is too short to waste so much time on the devil's play. By clearing the clutter, we can be more in tune with God. He wants us to want Him.

What are you missing out on by not receiving Christ? What miracles does God have in store for you? What is standing between you and Jesus? How can you use your story to inspire others? Are you going to heaven? How many of your loved ones will meet you there?

It all starts with giving your life to Jesus Christ. After that, He will show you the way. My husband and I are living proof.

So I Could Hear His Divine Messages

Now that I've shared my #savingstory, my spiritual awakening, and my experience with the miraculous recovery of my husband, I'd like to share one more thing. I want to talk about hearing God's messages. I believe He speaks to us every day, and it is our responsibility to listen. God will never forsake us. He never leaves us without the tools we need. In fact, He is consistently raining blessings down upon us. They're falling all around us, but are we taking advantage of His graciousness? We oftentimes choose to make our own plans and hear our own heart's desires. Instead, we must tune out this world's voice to hear His.

Just as important as receiving the messages, we must act on them. We've all heard the phrase, "Do it scared." God's path for us is not always the easiest path, but it is the path we must take. He gave me gifts that I have to use, even if I'm terrified of where they'll lead me. Writing this book, for example, was easy. The Holy Spirit guided me the entire way. The words flowed from my fingertips as they pressed the keys on my computer with enjoyable ease. It was my therapy. Publishing the book was the hard part because I was scared.

God commanded me to write a book about this experience, and so I did. Then I procrastinated for months because I was scared to reveal this story to the world. My publisher approved the manuscript for production, and I had one moment of celebration and then months of fear. The devil danced around me provoking thoughts of cancelling the project, but God's voice never wavered. Each day passed with self-doubt and disappointment that I hadn't signed the publishing agreement and submitted my final manuscript version.

Why? I feared any attention I would receive from this book. I feared that people would accuse me of seeking attention and glory.

I'm scared of any sort of media coverage or the possibility of speaking to groups about my story. I'm scared, period.

We have to do this scared.

As brothers and sisters in Christ, we make up His church body. Together, we are one. Each of us is given different attributes so as a whole, we are complete. Scripture directs us to be good stewards of our particular gifts to serve others for the glory of God. Well, folks, that's my purpose for sharing my story. I'm terrified of where this will lead me, but I don't have a choice. I am obeying God. Maybe this will lead me nowhere, and the whole project will be a failure. That's a fear too. If that's the case, I know God's lesson will be one that I need to learn. Regardless, I am called to share my gifts, and I hope you are too.

I need your gifts! We need each other. I hope this inspires you to not only seek out your God-given gifts but also to act on them. In my experience, living out God's will for me has led me closer to Him and His blessings.

Earlier, I mentioned about how God granted me anything I prayed for while we were in the hospital. It may sound trivial, but I prayed for warmth and was instantly warmed. Even with such a small request, God heard me. He hears us always, and we need to be listening to Him also. On that Thanksgiving Day in 2018, I asked myself what was next for our Christmas season. He immediately answered me.

One night, I was driving home right before dark. My headlights were on, but there was just enough daylight left to make seeing difficult. A feeling came over me that I should watch out for a deer. At that same moment, I saw something white bouncing up and down ahead on my lane. It was the tail of a baby deer lost and wandering down the road. My eyes were squinting, and my foot had risen off of my gas pedal. By the time I realized what was in the road, I mashed on my brakes and stopped just in time. I nearly mowed over a baby deer! Thankfully, I was in tune with God's message to slow down. He speaks to me with small and large messages, and I cherish them all.

Here's another instance of hearing, or rather, tasting God's message. I was speaking with my family about not taking God's name in vain. It's everywhere! It's all over movies and television, and it has become so common that I don't think people even realize what they're doing. Seriously, people, please stop saying, "Oh my God!" You're using our Creator's name with empty meaning. Our God deserves more respect than that. In our discussion, we went on to say that we shouldn't say, "Holy crap!" because nothing is truly holy, except God. I brought up the fact that I often say, "Holy moly." As I was speaking the words about how I probably shouldn't say that anymore, a bug flew in my mouth! Now if that wasn't a sign, I don't know what is.

Hearing our own personal messages from God is imperative to our participation in His ultimate plan, and by missing out on those messages, we are missing opportunities to work alongside Him.

Missing His message on November 22, 2018, would have been detrimental to my future. I am deeply thankful for that day, and I love how God chose Thanksgiving Day for my date of rebirth. If the date of Thanksgiving Day, November 22, doesn't seem ironic enough, let me share with you one more reason why that particular date is so significant. November 21 is the birthday of my ex-husband and the foster son I told you about earlier in this book. My first marriage and divorce, along with the time I spent as a foster parent, are two of the hardest times in my life. Those experiences are the ones I consider to be my largest failures. I felt as though I had disappointed God by that marriage and by failing as a foster parent.

On November 21, 2018, my struggle with those failures died because on that very next day, I was reborn again and reminded of God's grace. What a glorious message from God!

God speaks to me every day. Most often, it is through my heart. He lays advice and guidance on my heart as I pray to Him. He reveals messages as I read the Bible too. I'm a huge believer that we must read His Word every day.

The book of Daniel is one of my favorite books in the Holy Bible. Recalling the angelic visit that happened to me *three* days before nearly losing my husband, I constantly tried to decipher the full meaning of the message. I was visited *three* times. Why? Each time was shorter than the previous. Why? Chapter 10 in the book of Daniel lends to a theory I've worked up. God was sending me a message, but I wasn't quite sure how to decipher it.

The book of Daniel was one that I hadn't studied very much, but in the weeks before my angel encounter, I watched a *three*-part series about angels and demons (see the *Supernatural* series from The Rock Church Live Stream in Fenton, Michigan, from February 3, 10, and 17, 2019). My aunt had shared the sermons with me from her church, The Rock in Fenton, Michigan. That sermon sparked a lot of curiosity within me, but it would be months later before I would read Daniel and realize the similarities between the sermon, the book of Daniel, and my experience. I read the full book of Daniel and now understand the story in a different light.

It is human nature to see the world in a one-dimensional aspect, but there is another dimension that we don't see. There is a realm existing all around us where supernatural powers fight in an epic battle. In fact, Scripture tells us this, so I believe that we are surrounded by vicious fighting. My stomach turns when I think about how the devil's army is always near, working to corrupt God's plan. Humanity is in severe decline as the end of time nears, and our only hope is to find salvation in Jesus Christ. Two things are inevitably going to happen: your life will end, or time will end. Whichever way the end comes for you, the result is still the same. You will spend eternity somewhere. I take comfort in knowing that God always wins and that His angels, led by Jesus Christ, will conquer evil. Then I'll be spending my eternity in heaven. Anyone who isn't saved by the blood will be spending their eternity in hell.

> For we wrestle not against flesh and blood,
> but against principalities, against powers, against
> the rulers of the darkness of this world, against
> spiritual wickedness in high places. (Eph. 6:12)

The devil is real, and his demons are too. When Lucifer defied God, he took one-third of the angels with him. Think about that. It is hard to imagine that after being in the presence of God, anyone could take a notion to turn their backs on Him, but we all know how cunning the devil can be. Satan convinced one-third of the angels to leave God. He convinced one-third of the angels to engage in spiritual warfare, using mankind in his quest against God. We are being used, and by allowing yourself to be used, you are sacrificing your eternal life.

One-third of God's angels left the heavens and descended into inescapable peril. There is no way out for them now, so they continue to thrash and gnash with evilness, trying to take us down with them. That sounds intimidating, but do you know how many angels are still on God's side? The Bible doesn't reveal exactly how many angels God created, but it does give us the fact that there are too many for us to count. We are told that thousands upon thousands or even a myriad of angels are still on God's side.

One-third of them left heaven, but in reality, God is God. He can do anything. He is the great *I Am*! Sure, they joined Lucifer's brigade, but God is in control of all things, and He will win. We will win! Two-thirds of God's glorious angels are still present to protect, watch, and deliver messages to us (if we're listening), even though one-third of them switched sides. Since that time, the devil has used his minority in an effort to defeat the majority. We can read the book of Revelations to see how the story ends.

Back to Daniel, Daniel had been praying to God for under-standing. He states himself, "In those days I Daniel was mourning *three* full weeks" (Dan. 10:2; italics added). He goes on to explain how he had been preparing to receive God's word. He had been fervently preparing and praying for over *three* weeks with seemingly no response from God, but then the loyal and dedicated Daniel received the acknowledgement he had been searching for.

And I Daniel alone saw the vision. (Dan. 10:7)

Sound familiar? Daniel was not alone at the time of the visit, but he was the only one to see the vision. Similarly, I was not alone during my encounters, but I was the only one to see the visions.

Therefore I was left alone and saw this great
vision, and there remained no strength in me:
for my vigor was turned in me into frailty, and I
retained no strength. (Dan. 10:8)

I too had no strength during my angelic visit. But wait, there's more. Let's read on to see how the angel explains why his arrival took so long.

> Then said he unto me, Fear not, Daniel. For from the first day that thou didst set thine heart to understand, and to humble thyself before thy God, thy words were heard, and I am come for thy words.
>
> But the prince of the kingdom of Persia withstood me one and twenty days: but, lo, Michael, one of the chief princes, came to help me; and I remained there with the kings of Persia. (Dan. 10:12–13)

The prince of the kingdom of Persia refers to a demon, and that demon had been holding the angel (most likely Gabriel) back from visiting Daniel. The angel fought for *three* weeks, and then Michael, the archangel, came to help.

One theory I have as to why I encountered my most recent angelic visit in *three* phases is that a demon was there battling my angel in an effort to stop the message.

My faith is strong on its own, but I am unsure of how I could've handled the stress of almost losing my husband without the undoubted message from God that He would stay with me throughout my adversity. The devil definitely wasn't happy about me receiving that message of comfort from God.

During the three months of preparation, I had committed to God's plan for me. I was unaware of exactly what lay ahead of me, but I knew something was coming. I was committed to enduring adversity, leaning on Him, and doing whatever it takes to spread His glory. That angelic visit left me with the knowledge that God would be with me through anything and everything. Without that, the faith of our loved ones, and our fervent prayer and dedication to God's will during that time in the hospital, I do not believe my husband would still be here with us today; thus, I would not be sharing this glorious story.

God would have missed out on the praise, and you would have missed out on this story, and the devil would have had his way.

I know it sounds complicated, but I believe this. I believe that good comes from all tragedy, and God uses tough times to increase our faith and the faith of those around us.

Another theory I developed from the book of Daniel is this:

> Yet I heard the voice of his words; and when I heard the voice of his words, then was I in a deep sleep on my face, and my face toward the ground.
>
> And, behold, a hand touched me, which set me upon my knees and upon the palms of my hands.
>
> And he said unto me, O Daniel, a man greatly beloved, understand the words that I speak unto thee, and stand upright; for unto thee am I now sent. And when he had spoken this word unto me, I stood trembling. (Dan. 10:9–11)

The angel called Daniel "beloved," which sparked an interest in me because my name, Amy, means "beloved." There is yet another meaningful detail that God used to catch my attention.

Here, we see that Daniel had lost all strength at the sight of the angel; but through the messenger, God sent power to Daniel so he could stand. Then,

> And when he had spoken such words unto me, I set my face toward the ground, and I became dumb.
>
> And, behold, one like the similitude of the sons of men touched my lips: then I opened my mouth, and spake, and said unto him that stood before me, O my lord, by the vision my sorrows

are turned upon me, and I have retained no strength.

For how can the servant of this my lord talk with this my lord? For as for me, straightway there remained no strength in me, neither is there breath left in me.

Then there came again and touched me one like the appearance of a man, and he strengthened me. (Dan. 10:15–18)

Here, we see that Daniel was physically strengthened two more times during this encounter for a total of *three* times. I believe that the angel who visited me sent me a message of strength from God, and he delivered it to me *three* times. Without the mental, physical, and spiritual strengthening, I would not have been able to lift my 230-pound husband and perform chest compressions for six minutes, all while maintaining composure in front of our daughter, managing two phone conversations, calming and watching our daughter throughout the duration, and then immediately start praying and starting prayer chains via text messages. There was absolutely no way I could have done that without the strength from God. Not only was I able to complete those stressful tasks during the actual emergency, I was also able to stand strong in my faith throughout the unknowns and adversity I would face during our stay at the hospital and beyond during our at-home recovery. All the glory goes to God!

The book of Daniel is a thrilling look into the spiritual realm.

Am I comparing myself to Daniel? No, absolutely not. I am so not worthy of any praise and definitely not worthy of comparison to Daniel or any biblical person, but I found comfort in the passages within the book of Daniel and appreciate the insight that the Living Word provided me for this and other circumstances. I'm using my understanding of the book of Daniel as an example of how we can receive messages via the Living Word. I hope you feel the same and that you find your own comfort and guidance from Scripture.

By now, surely, you've noticed how many times the number *three* has appeared in my testimony. I believe that God has made the number *three* relevant in my story to draw attention to the sheer awesomeness of His miracle. I believe that my story alone would inspire others, but with so many occurrences of the number *three*, my story takes on an undeniable attraction. It is clear that God had His hand on this story. After all, God made His presence known and is now using me to spread the message of salvation. I'm here to win souls for our awesome God!

When we think about numbers in the Bible, seven, forty, and *three* come to mind. The number *three* occurs in the Holy Bible hundreds of times. Symbolizing divine emphasis, the number *three* also directs us to recognize wholeness, completeness, and perfection. The number three is used biblically to highlight intensity.

As the miracle of my husband's recovery was happening, the number *three* came up over and over again, and I quickly realized that God had orchestrated every detail. I believe with every shred of my being that He brought us through everything with the intention that I would use the story to lead others to Christ. God uses adversity to get our attention and prepare us for service. On November 21, 2018, I didn't understand my purpose. I felt somewhat empty and meaningless. What a difference a day makes! On that beautiful Thanksgiving Day, November 22, 2018, my sense of direction changed; and a spark of desire to lead others to Christ was lit within my heart. I've been blessed beyond measure to have the opportunity to share my story with you.

How could anyone deny these facts? Our miracle started with an angelic message from God that occurred in *three* consecutive visits. Then,

- *Three* days later, my husband's heart stopped beating.
- *Three* paramedics arrived at our home.
- The paramedics shocked my husband's heart *three* times.
- My husband was in a coma for *three* days.
- On the *third* day, he opened his eyes.

- I heard *three* LIFESTAR helicopters land over me while in the hospital.
- *Three* days after waking up, my husband received a pacemaker/defibrillator.
- My husband's recovery took *three* months, and then he was able to return to work.

There are other occurrences of the number *three* in my story, but these prove to be most relevant. It is purely amazing for me to reminisce about the number *three* in my story, but the most amazing occurrence of all of them is the fact that my husband's heart stopped exactly *three* months from that Thanksgiving Day, when God softened my heart to the changes I needed to make in my life. What if I had missed that message? I started making changes immediately, and He continued to prepare me for *three* months. For *three* months, I grew closer to Him. I made it through the adversity with lessons learned and increased spiritual strength. I continue to grow into the woman God intends me to be, but for those *three* months, I experienced rapid and awe-inspiring growth. I became more aware of what I was doing and what I wanted to do. All of this was possible simply by listening and obeying our Creator.

The changes I made during those *three* months will have a lasting impact in my life, as well as my husband's and daughter's lives. Now that you've finished this book, my hope is that this story inspires you to further seek God. With God, we are an unstoppable force! What if this world was filled with a greater quantity of powerful and relentless soldiers fighting for God? I pray that reading my testimony will spark a flame within you too or will strengthen your flame and that you'll share this book with a loved one when you're done.

This story is for everyone. It's for spouses who want to focus on their dedication to each other by seeking support from the Holy Spirit. It's for parents who want a brighter future for their children. It's for grandparents who pray for their family's love and dedication to Christ. It's for friends who pray that their loved ones will walk with the Holy Spirit. It is for anyone who needs to be strengthened physically, mentally, and spiritually by the only One who truly knows how to—our Creator. Most of all, this book is for the souls in this world who are lost, who are without the salvation of Jesus Christ, and who need to be strengthened to complete their spiritual potential. Without accepting Jesus Christ, we are capable of nothing. We may think we are, but once you've received Him, you will see this life differently and will understand how empty your life was before the gift of the Holy Spirit.

You Will Never Find a Better Love

Your husband, he left
And your boyfriend cheated
And your sister won't answer her phone
Your mama, she meddles
And your daddy forgets
And your best friend left you alone
He is there; He's still there
And He's with you everywhere

You will never find a better love
You will never find a better love
You will never find a better love
He loves you just because

Even when you collapse on the bottom
Your hand can reach the top
He can lift you from the depths
Of whatever's going on
You will never find a better love

Your husband, he left
And your boyfriend cheated
And your sister won't answer her phone
Your mama, she meddles
And your daddy forgets

And your best friend left you alone
He is there; He's still there
And He's with you everywhere

You will never find a better love
You will never find a better love
You will never find a better love
He loves you just because

Just because you pledged your life to Him
Just because you're convicted of your sins
Just because you love Him again and again
He loves you; oh, He loves you
He loves you just because

Your husband, he left
And your boyfriend cheated
And your sister won't answer her phone
Your mama, she meddles
And your daddy forgets
And your best friend left you alone
He is there; He's still there
And He's with you everywhere

You will never find a better love
You will never find a better love
You will never find a better love
He loves you just because

This book was meant to ignite a spark within the hearts of those who struggle with clutter or who need to be saved from the death of this world. Maybe you're already saved, but you're still drowning in a sea of clutter. Can you clear the clutter and hear God's messages? Is it time for a rebirth? I also pray that this book will inspire you to lead someone else to Christ. This story is for everyone. It is for every single soul on earth, so if you happen to know someone other than yourself, please share this book with them when you're finished.

Friends don't let friends live a cluttered life!

With every act and every word, I strive to ask myself, "Does this honor God?" If the answer is no, I work to change myself so I can glorify Him more. If the answer is yes, I smile and praise Him because He changed me into someone who loves to praise Him. I'm not perfect, but He is, and He considers me worthy. He considers *you* worthy too.

> Jesus answered and said unto him, If a man love me, he will keep my words: and my Father will love him, and we will come unto him, and make our abode with him.
>
> He that loveth me not keepeth not my sayings: and the word which ye hear is not mine, but the Father's which sent me.
>
> These things have I spoken unto you, being yet present with you.
>
> But the Comforter, which is the Holy Ghost, whom the father will send in my name, he shall teach you all things, and bring all things to your rememberance, whatsoever I have said unto you.
>
> Peace I leave with you, my peace I give unto you: not as the world giveth, give I unto you. Let not your heart be troubled, neither let it be afraid. (John 14:23–27)

By the Way

By the way, He speaks to me
And by the way, I speak to Him
By the way, He changed my life
I live, and I'll live again

By the way, have I told you that on that joyous day
I want to see your soul in heaven, and you can get there, by the way
By the way, Jesus told us to follow him; we can go
But the way, it's straight and narrow. Will you join me, by the way?

By the way, He loves His children
And by the way, He sent His Son
By the way, He gave salvation
I live, and I'll live again

By the way, have I told you that on that joyous day
I want to see your soul in heaven, and you can get there, by the way
By the way, Jesus told us to follow him; we can go
But the way, it's straight and narrow. Will you join me, by the way?

About the Author

Fueled by God's grace and strengthened by the Holy Spirit, Amy Morton is on a mission to win souls in the name of Jesus Christ.

Born in Flint, Michigan, and raised in the charming Southern Appalachian town of Dandridge, Tennessee, Amy is a proud graduate of Jefferson County High School, Walters State Community College, and Lincoln Memorial University. She stepped back from a marketing career that spanned over a decade in the exciting Smoky Mountain tourism industry to stay at home with her daughter full-time. That move would essentially spark a series of life changes leading up to the events that inspired her to write *Because He Saved Me*. After she witnessed the unfolding miracle of how God used her to save her husband's life, Amy became faithfully devoted to spreading God's glory. Amy strives to continually grow into the expectation that God has set for her and purposefully seeks ways to similarly inspire others.

Along with her husband and daughter, Amy is a member of Lyons Creek Baptist Church in Strawberry Plains, Tennessee. They live just outside of Knoxville and enjoy living a simple lifestyle and raising their daughter to also be a devoted follower of Jesus Christ.

CPSIA information can be obtained
at www.ICGtesting.com
Printed in the USA
LVHW031359311220
675393LV00006B/914